Reel Rangers

Texas Rangers in Movies, TV, Radio,
and Other Forms of Popular Culture

Bill O'Neal

EAKIN PRESS Fort Worth, Texas
www.EakinPress.com

With love for my vivacious daughter
Dr. Berri O'Neal Gormley

Except for credited photographs, the illustrations in this book
are from the author's collection.

Copyright © 2008
By Bill O'Neal
Published By Eakin Press
An Imprint of Wild Horse Media Group
P.O. Box 331779
Fort Worth, Texas 76163
1-817-344-7036
www.EakinPress.com
ALL RIGHTS RESERVED
1 2 3 4 5 6 7 8 9
ISBN-10: 1-57168-840-4
ISBN-13: 978-1-57168-840-8
Library of Congress Control Number 2004110075

Contents

John Wayne as Texas Ranger Captain Jake Cutter in The Comancheros.

Introduction

*"Lord, we send Thy way this day a lowly sinner who lost his way.
Thou send him to Heaven or Hell, it is for Thee to judge. We are
done with him. Amen."*
> —Ranger captain Burmeister over the grave
> of a bad guy in Elmer Kelton's
> *The Way of the Coyote*

"Ain't no one ever killed no Texas Ranger and lived to tell it."
> —Bad guy in *Lone Wolf McQuade*

"We're Rangers, men. We've got right on our side!"
> —Captain Leander McNelly in
> the 2001 movie, *Texas Rangers*

"Ride, Ranger, ride,
You have conquered every foe
Since a hundred years ago,
Ride, Ranger, ride.
> —Theme song for Gene Autry's
> *Ride, Ranger, Ride*

*T*he systematic exploration of the popular culture of Texas
Rangers has brought me a deep and nostalgic pleasure.
As a boy during the late 1940s, I rarely missed a radio episode
of *The Lone Ranger*, and later I became a devoted fan of *Tales
of the Texas Rangers*. During the late 1950s, enamored of

Western movies, I saw a great many Ranger films on big and small screens, and my love affair with cinema has proved to be lifelong. For more than two decades, while regularly conducting Traveling Texas History classes for Panola College in Carthage, I guided hundreds of students through the Texas Ranger Hall of Fame and Museum in Waco, as well as to other Ranger sites around the Lone Star State. With the proliferation on video of old movies and TV programs, I realized that a rich and varied collection of Ranger culture is available, to be viewed or read about or visited.

A number of people aided with my search for materials and information. Bobby Nieman of Longview, official oral historian of the Texas Rangers, shared his intimate knowledge of Rangers and Ranger events of the past few decades. I am grateful to Judy Shofner and Christina Stopka, at the research library at the Texas Ranger Hall of Fame and Museum, for their efficient response to my several queries for assistance. Chuck Parsons of Luling, noted Ranger author and researcher, told me of the location of statuary of which I was unaware. Charles Johnston, a friend from Los Angeles who is an expert on Western movies, graciously provided several needed videos.

One of my daughters, Dr. Berri O'Neal of Dallas, offered welcome assistance with photography and Internet research. My longtime editor, Melissa Locke Roberts, improved the manuscript with her customary expertise and cheerful tact. My wife, Karon, helped with research and photography, graciously permitted me to spend hour after hour viewing videos, prepared the final manuscript, and provided welcome encouragement and insightful suggestions throughout the project.

I am indebted to everyone who helped me follow the cultural trail of the Texas Rangers. I welcome the readers who are

ready to join me on that trail with a quote from the most famous fictional Ranger of all:

"Hi-yo, Silver, away . . ."

The Lone Ranger (Clayton Moore) and Silver.

1910s–1920s:
Rangers on the Silent Screen

"Gentlemen,—I have the honor to dedicate this book to you, and the hope that it shall fall my lot to tell the world about a strange, unique, and misunderstood body of men—the Texas Rangers— who made the great Lone Star State habitable, who never know peaceful rest and sleep, who are passing, who surely will not be forgotten and will some day come into their own."
                                   —Zane Grey, *The Lone Star Ranger*

From *The Lone Ranger* to *Walker, Texas Ranger*, from Zane Grey's *The Lone Star Ranger* to Larry McMurtry's *Lonesome Dove*, Texas Rangers have been portrayed on the silver screen, network radio, and television. John Wayne, Gary Cooper, Tom Mix, Clint Eastwood, Gene Autry, Roy Rogers, and a host of lesser Western stars each took his turn at depicting Texas Rangers. For nearly a century the world's most famous law enforcement body has inspired Western novelists, actors and filmmakers.

The Western motion picture formula was established by *The Great Train Robbery* in 1903. *The Great Train Robbery* spawned numerous imitations and produced the first Western movie star. G. M. Anderson (born Max Aronson in 1882) appeared in the nine-minute movie, convincing director Edwin S. Porter "that he could ride any horse as well as a Texas

1

Ranger," according to film historian Jon Tuska. A couple of years would pass before Anderson learned to ride, but he became a director in the fledgling film industry on the strength of his association with *The Great Train Robbery*.

Anderson and George Spoor, a distributor for screen equipment, founded a film company called Essanay Studios (the gifted comedian Charles Chaplain soon would be signed by Essanay). Hoping to create a Western series around an identifiable hero, Anderson purchased screen rights to a *Saturday Evening Post* short story featuring a character named Broncho Billy. When he could not find a suitable actor, Anderson assumed the role of Broncho Billy. Although he was not handsome, Anderson's sturdy physique was convincing in fight scenes. The southern California settings were impressive on nickelodeon screens, while Anderson's simple costumes and sets were true to a West which remained readily in evidence during the early years of the twentieth century.

Broncho Billy Westerns proved immediately popular. Anderson filmed one Broncho Billy movie per week, and some urban theaters ran these one- and two-reelers (approximately ten or twenty minutes) exclusively. Anderson often included his hero's name in the titles: *Broncho Billy's Redemption*, *Broncho Billy and the Schoolmistress*, *Broncho Billy's Vengeance*, etc. Anderson released 375 short Westerns from 1908 through 1915, although a majority of these films have been destroyed by nitrate decomposition.

For several years Anderson reigned as filmdom's first Western star. He played Rangers at least twice, in *The Ranger's Bride* (1910), and *The Border Ranger* (1911). It is likely that with his prolific output, Anderson included Ranger portrayals in other films.

The first cowboy star, Broncho Billy Anderson, played a Texas Ranger at least twice.

With the popular Broncho Billy Anderson wearing a Ranger badge onscreen, Selig Studios followed suit, featuring William Duncan in *The Ranger and His Horse* (1912). The athletic Duncan was Selig's principal action star, headlining twenty-three short films—mostly Westerns—in 1912. Duncan frequently directed his own films, including *The Ranger and His Horse*. Myrtle Stedman, as usual, played Duncan's romantic interest.

Another player who often was featured opposite Duncan and Stedman—although not in *The Ranger and His Horse*—was future superstar Tom Mix. Born in 1880, Mix was the same age as Duncan. In 1898 the eighteen-year-old Mix enlisted in the army during the Spanish-American War. He never left the United States, but Mix rose to the rank of sergeant and re-enlisted in 1901. The next year Sergeant Mix married, then deserted the army and took his bride to Oklahoma Territory. The couple did not remain together, and a second marriage also was brief. But Mix stayed in Oklahoma, working as a bartender, then as a town marshal in Dewey. Soon he became associated with the nearby 101 Ranch, a pioneer Oklahoma spread which had become a nationally popular guest ranch. The 101 toured a large Wild West Show, and Tom Mix soon became a performer. He married a female performer, then gravitated into the movies.

Late in 1913 Selig Studios gave Mix the lead in his own series of short Westerns. Mix stressed action, humor and romance, and his horse Old Blue (later replaced by Tony) was given star billing. A big, talented athlete with dark good looks, Mix was an exciting presence onscreen. To exalt his image, he claimed to have been born in El Paso (instead of Mix Run, Pennsylvania), to have served as a Texas Ranger and a United

States marshal, and to have charged up San Juan Hill. The Tom Mix publicity connection to Texas Rangers soon would translate to celluloid.

In 1914 Selig Studios released forty-eight Tom Mix movies, including, on October 15, *The Ranger's Romance*. Mix directed the one-reeler, and the cast included regular co-stars Goldie Coldwell and Roy Watson, along with Old Blue. As the star of Tom Mix rose in the Hollywood firmament, he would make a quartet of far more significant Ranger movies.

Concurrent with the growing public appetite for Western films was the soaring popularity of Western novelist Zane Grey. The former dentist began writing early in the twentieth century, and he became captivated with the West during a trip to collect background material. *Riders of the Purple Sage*, published by Harper & Brothers in 1912, was enormously successful. The central character, a deadly gunman named Jim Lassiter, was a former Texas Ranger who had come to Utah in pursuit of his sister's killer. Lassiter comes to the aid of rancher Jane Withersteen, and the couple engages in a boldly romantic ending. The novel became an instant Western classic, ex-Ranger Lassiter remains one of the most memorable of all Western heroes, and *Riders of the Purple Sage* has been filmed five times.

In 1913 Grey made his first visit to Texas to investigate the Rangers. In San Antonio he met with legendary Ranger Captain John Hughes, who had battled lawbreakers since 1887. (Hughes would retire in 1915.) Grey also traveled along the border with other Rangers, including "the giant [Jeff] Vaughn" and Joe Sitters, who was killed in a 1916 ambush. The author was deeply impressed by the men who wore the badge. By this time the Texas Rangers were famous for combat

against Comanche and Kiowa war parties and, more recently, for battling rustlers, bank and train robbers, and feudists. But by the end of the nineteenth century outlawry in Texas had been greatly curtailed. In 1901 the Legislature reduced the Ranger force to four companies of no more than twenty men each (the Frontier Battalion had been organized in 1874 with six companies of seventy-five men each). But in 1910 the Mexican Revolution erupted, increasing tensions on both sides of the border. With a reduced force, Rangers often found themselves riding alone in dangerous country, as Grey learned during his visit.

Zane Grey in 1918 on the set of the first film version of Riders of the Purple Sage.

Captivated by the historic adventures of the Rangers, as well as by the continuing risks of contemporary service, Grey became particularly intrigued by Captain L. H. McNelly. Although McNelly died of tuberculosis in 1877 at thirty-two, he became a legend in Texas as a Confederate officer, leader of the State Police, and captain of a special Ranger force. Soon Grey began writing the adventures of Buck Duane, a fugitive gunman who became a Texas Ranger and was given a series of dangerous assignments by Captain McNelly.

"The Lone Star Ranger" appeared in serial form in *All Star Cavalier Weekly* beginning in May 1914, while "The Last of the Duanes" came out in *Argosy Magazine* in September 1914. *The Lone Star Ranger*, combining the first half of "The Last of the Duanes" and the last half of "The Lone Star Ranger," was published as a novel in 1915 and quickly became a best-seller. Several actors would portray Buck Duane in various film versions of *The Lone Star Ranger* and *The Last of the Duanes*.

While Grey was bringing Texas Rangers Jim Lassiter and Buck Duane to the world of Western fiction, Ranger movies continued to flicker on the screens of thousands of new theaters in America. In 1916 a twenty-chapter serial was released, *Liberty, A Daughter of the U.S.A.* Marie Walcamp played the title role, while rugged Jack Holt co-starred as a Texas Ranger in the first Western serial ever filmed. For twenty weeks young audiences were thrilled by Ranger Holt in such chapters as "The Fangs of the Wolf," "Riding with Death," and "A Trail of Blood." Action star Holt, who later would portray detective Dick Tracy, had a son and daughter, and when they were grown both Tim Holt and Jennifer Holt would be featured in Ranger films.

Zane Grey's Ranger Movies

The immensely popular and prolific Zane Grey produced eighty-nine books. Fifty-six were Western novels, and with millions of readers it was inevitable that Grey's frontier romances would be brought to the silver screen. In 1916 studio head William Fox paid Grey $2,500 apiece for movie rights to *Riders of the Purple Sage* and *The Light of Western Stars*. After these novels were filmed and released a couple of years later, Grey established a rights fee of $25,000, a sensational sum for the time. Grey also insisted that each contract include an unprecedented seven-year lease, so that he could sell the property again. Indeed, many of his novels were filmed more than once, for a staggering total of 109 Zane Grey movies to date.

A number of these films involved Texas Ranger characters, often portrayed by the popular George O'Brien or by superstar Tom Mix. *Riders of the Purple Sage* was filmed in 1918, 1925, 1931, 1941, and 1995. A sequel, *The Rainbow Trail*, was filmed in 1925 and 1932. *The Lone Star Ranger* was lensed in 1919, 1923, and 1930. *The Dude Ranger*, published in 1930 in serial form (and in 1951 as a novel), was filmed in 1934. *The Last of the Duanes* was made into a movie four times, 1919, 1924, 1930 and 1941. Zane Grey and the Texas Rangers provided an exciting combination for moviegoers.

Other Ranger movies of this era included *The Ranger of Lonesome Gulch* (1916), *The Ranger* (1918), and *Heart of the Southwest* (1918). By this time (1918) the first film version of *Riders of the Purple Sage* was released by William Fox, who had bought motion picture rights to the hit novel two years earlier. William Farnum played Lassiter, while future cowboy star Buck Jones had a small part in the six-reel movie.

The following year Farnum played Buck Duane in the first version of *The Lone Star Ranger*, and also in 1919 *The Last of the Duanes* was filmed for the first time. That same year *Jim of the Rangers* was released, and *The Unknown Ranger* came out in 1920. In 1921 *The Ranger and the Law* and *The Sky Ranger* offered Ranger adventure to moviegoers, and so did *The Big Ranger* and *The Ranger's Reward* in 1922. Early in 1923 the muscular and stalwart Buck Jones starred in *Footlight Ranger*, a Fox five-reeler.

Also in 1923 Fox remade *The Lone Star Ranger*, with Western star Tom Mix as Buck Duane. The eight-reel film was well over an

WILLIAM FOX
PRESENTS

WILLIAM FARNUM

ZANE GREY'S Dramatic Story

THE LONE STAR RANGER

A ROMANCE OF THE GREAT SOUTHWEST
DIRECTION BY J GORDON EDWARDS
STANDARD PICTURES   FOX FILM CORPORATION

Lobby card from the first of three film versions of The Lone Star Ranger *(1919).*

Only four years passed before Fox remade The Lone Star Ranger, *with superstar Tom Mix in one of his several Ranger roles.*

hour long. Mix was the most popular cowboy hero of the 1920s, earning $17,000 a week. The profitable combination of Tom Mix and Zane Grey was a horse Fox would continue to ride. In 1924 Mix starred in a remake of *The Last of the Duanes*.

The following year Fox remade *Riders of the Purple Sage*, with Tom Mix as Lassiter. In this six-reel version, Texas Ranger Jim Lassiter vows revenge on lawyer Lew Walters, who has abducted his sister and her daughter. During his search he encounters Jane Withersteen and, finally, Walters, now known as Judge Dyer. Judge Dyer, played by Warner Oland (who would earn screen fame as Charlie Chan), is shot to death by the implacable Lassiter. When chased by a posse toward remote Paradise Valley, Lassiter and Jane realize the depth of their love. Lassiter dislodges a boulder that cuts off the posse but seals the couple inside Paradise Valley.

Fox immediately filmed a sequel with Tom Mix. *The Rainbow Trail* hit movie screens—there were 20,000 American movie theaters by the mid-1920s—in May 1925, two months after the release of *Riders of the Purple Sage*. Another actor played Jim Lassiter, because this time Mix starred as Lassiter's nephew, John Shefford. Shefford vanquishes the bad guys who had survived Lassiter, while finding romance with Jane's adopted daughter. Shefford also frees Lassiter and Jane from Paradise Valley, and the couple at last is married.

The recent spate of Ranger movies starring Tom Mix spawned a flurry of Ranger films with lesser cowboy actors. Before 1925 had ended theaters ran *The Fighting Ranger* (with Charles Avery and Slim Cole), *One Shot Ranger* (Pete Morrison), *Ranger of the Big Pines* and *Ranger Bill*. In 1926

Western superstar Tom Mix played a Ranger in several films, and for publicity purposes he claimed to have served as a Texas Ranger while he was a young man. In his final role, the serial The Miracle Rider *(1935), Mix played a Texas Ranger captain.*

Ahead of the Law featured a Texas Ranger character, and so did *The Fighting Ranger*, a five-reeler starring Al Hoxie. Al's more famous brother, Jack Hoxie, starred in *Rambling Ranger* in 1927. Also in 1927 Tom Mix—and Tony—returned to the Ranger theme in *Outlaws of Red River*, a six-reel "Drama of the Fighting Texas Ranger." Of course, the claim of Tom Mix that he had worn a Ranger badge as a young man remained prominent in his publicity.

Al Hoxie was back in 1928 with *The Ranger's Oath*. Other Ranger movies of the 1920s included *Law of the Ranger*, *The Four-Footed Ranger* and *The Phantom Flyer*. *Rio Rita* in 1929 starred Bebe Daniels in the title role, while James Stewart (not the lanky actor who would become an American icon) played a Texas Ranger captain. The Ranger captain pursues an outlaw called "The Kinkajou" across the Rio Grande into Mexico, where he falls in love with Rita.

By this time the end was in sight for silent Westerns. In 1927 Al Jolson electrified movie audiences by singing several songs in *The Jazz Singer*. Although title cards were used for dialogue, Jolson also recorded a few spoken words on the sound track. Audiences demanded talking films, and as studios responded attendance exploded, from 60 million during 1927 to 110 million in 1929. Westerns were slow to convert to sound because of concerns about recording outdoor dramas. But in 1929 director Raoul Walsh filmed a Cisco Kid adventure, *In Old Arizona*, successfully recording not only dialogue, but gunshots, galloping hoofbeats, and even the sound of bacon sizzling in a frying pan. The song *My Tonia* became a hit record, inspiring cowboy star Ken Maynard to experiment with a singing cowboy concept.

Silent Westerns had regularly presented Texas Ranger ad-

ventures to movie fans. The most popular Western star of the silent era, Tom Mix, had portrayed Rangers in a number of films. Silent movies established a Texas Ranger theme that audiences would expect to be continued in sound Westerns.

The Silent Era

BEST RANGER MOVIES
Liberty (1916—first Western serial, with Jack Holt as Texas Ranger)
The Lone Star Ranger (1923—Tom Mix)
The Last of the Duanes (1924—Tom Mix)
Riders of the Purple Sage (1925—Tom Mix)

BEST RANGER BOOK
The Lone Star Ranger (1915—Zane Grey)

BEST RANGER MAGAZINE SERIAL
"The Last of the Duanes," *Argosy* (1914—Zane Grey)

RANGER EVENTS
Rangers, along with hundreds of "Special Rangers," engage in murderous violence on the Mexican border (1914-1919).
Force Reduction—four companies not to exceed 15 men apiece (1919).
Tried to curb bootlegging during Prohibition, control KKK demonstrations, and keep order in oil boomtowns (1920s)

MOST FAMOUS RANGERS
Captain John R. Hughes, "The Border Boss"
Captain Bill McDonald, "One Riot, One Ranger"
Captain Frank Hamer
Captain Tom Hickman

1930s: The Masked Man and Other Talking Rangers

"A fiery horse with the speed of light, a cloud of dust and a hearty Hi-Yo Silver! The Lone Ranger rides again."
—Announcer, *The Lone Ranger*

During the depression decade, the Texas Rangers were threatened by budget slashes, political opponents, and the merger of the force into a newly formed Department of Public Safety. But while the Rangers struggled to maintain their identity and very existence during the 1930s, the Ranger image flourished in the popular media. Talking motion pictures, the celebration of the Texas Centennial, and a sensational hit on network radio promoted a valiant Ranger image to the American public.

In 1930 popular cowboy star Ken Maynard made *The Fighting Legion* for Universal Studios. As a young man he worked in Wild West shows, served in World War I, and won $42,000 as the World's All-Around Champion Cowboy. Persuaded by Tom Mix and Buck Jones to visit Hollywood, Maynard quickly became a star of silent Westerns. Ken Maynard films soon enjoyed big budgets, and *The Fighting Legion* was feature length, running an hour and fifteen minutes. But it also was silent, although one version had a little

sound, including a rowdy saloon song by the three "Hook brothers." The opening scene finds "Dave Hayes" (Maynard) and his sidekick fleeing "from the long arm of ranger law" in the person of Ranger Tom Dawson. But Dawson is spilled into a river during the pursuit, and the good-badmen ride back to pull him to safety. Dawson in turn lets them go free. Then Dawson is ambushed, and Maynard takes his badge (a shield with "TEXAS" engraved across the front and topped by an eagle) and vows revenge. Maynard leads his sidekick to lawless Bowden, where Dawson was about to establish a Ranger office. During a saloon brawl ("I always figure a good fight's the best way to get acquainted," smiles Maynard) the badge drops from Ken's pocket. Maynard is thought to be Ranger Dawson, and he assumes the role of lawman and cleans up the town. In the end the Ranger captain pins the badge on the hero: "Dave Hayes, you're now a Texas Ranger—a member of the Fighting Legion." But *The Fighting Legion* would be the last silent film about Rangers.

In 1930 Fox Studios remade *The Lone Star Ranger*, billed as "The First Zane Grey All-Talking Picture." The star was muscular, athletic George O'Brien. One of the busiest cowboy heroes of the 1930s, O'Brien would make several excellent Ranger movies. Born in 1900, he excelled in boxing and baseball before joining the navy during World War I (O'Brien would leave the movies during World War II to re-enlist in the navy). At Santa Clara State College he was attracted to dramatics, and a chance meeting with Tom Mix led to bit parts at Fox. In 1924 director John Ford cast the unknown O'Brien to star in *The Iron Horse*, which became a Western classic of the silent era. The handsome young actor enjoyed a succession of varied roles. In 1930 Fox decided to star O'Brien in a series of

Before going to Hollywood, Ken Maynard was a Wild West show performer, World War I veteran, and rodeo champion. After being mistaken for a Texas Ranger in The Fighting Legion, *Ken donned a huge white hat to indicate his transformation from marginal bad guy to lawman.*

Westerns that had strong budgets, shooting schedules of one month or more, and scenic locations in Colorado, Montana, and Utah.

The first of these fine movies was the third version of *The Lone Star Ranger* (the silent versions had been filmed in 1919 and 1923). O'Brien was effective as the outlaw turned Ranger trying to earn a pardon after falling in love with a girl from the East. Then Fox remade *Last of the Duanes*, also released in 1930. As Buck Duane, O'Brien tries to rescue the heroine from an outlaw leader, while being romanced by the outlaw's wife (Myrna Loy, who graduated from supporting roles to stardom within five years). Finally Buck is able to turn the gang leader over to Texas Rangers. (Fox simultaneously filmed a Spanish version, *Ultimo de Los Vargos*, starring George Lewis and Luana Alcaniz.)

George O'Brien continued to specialize in hour-long Westerns, making several Zane Grey films. In 1931 O'Brien became the third actor to portray vengeance-minded Ranger Jim Lassiter in the first sound version of *Riders of the Purple Sage*. Noah Berry played the crooked judge, while lovely Marguerite Churchill was Jane Withersteen. In 1925 Tom Mix had immediately followed *Riders of the Purple Sage* with Zane Grey's sequel, *The Rainbow Trail*, and Fox used the same pattern with O'Brien. Like Mix in 1925, O'Brien played Lassiter's nephew. Photography of *The Rainbow Trail* was superb, with locations in the Grand Canyon.

The busy O'Brien did not make another Ranger film until 1934, when he starred in Zane Grey's *The Dude Ranger*. O'Brien was an Easterner who inherited rustling along with a cattle ranch. But the movie stressed ranching scenes and comedy more than gunplay.

George O'Brien and Myrna Loy in Last of the Duanes. *During the 1930s O'Brien starred in five Ranger movies.*

In 1936 O'Brien was signed by RKO to make Westerns for $21,000 per film, which made him the screen's highest paid cowboy hero (until 1938, when William Boyd received a raise to $25,000 for each Hopalong Cassidy film). In 1938 RKO placed O'Brien in *The Renegade Ranger*, a remake of their 1932 release, *Come On Danger!* O'Brien is a Ranger assigned to bring Rita Hayworth, a female Robin Hood unjustly accused of murder. Young Tim Holt quits the Rangers to help her organize the homesteaders to battle against rustlers and crooked politicians. Beautiful and vivacious, the twenty-year-old Hayworth was given as much screen time as O'Brien. She rode

horseback skillfully, and on her feet "she was poetry in motion," stated O'Brien of the future superstar.

While George O'Brien portrayed Rangers during the 1930s, other Western stars took their turn as celluloid Rangers. In *Border Law* (1930), Buck Jones is a Texas Ranger who takes a leave of absence to pursue the gang that killed his brother during a holdup. Masquerading as the "Pecos Kid," Buck is befriended by the gang leader—who later is pummeled by Jones in a rousing brawl. Buck's silent movie fans were elated at the improvement that sound made in his performances. Indeed, Buck Jones benefited more from talkies than any other silent cowboy actor, and through the mid-1930s he reigned as the most popular Western star. As many as five million youngsters joined his fan club, the Buck Jones Rangers. Periodically, Buck, astride his magnificent horse, Silver, would embody his Ranger connection by starring as a Texas lawman.

One of his finest films was *The Texas Ranger* (1931). After being forced off her land, the heroine turns to banditry to get even. Ranger Jones masquerades as an outlaw to gain her confidence, then reveals his true identity. Amid the comic touches Buck's fans expected, the heroine helped him round up the real bad guys. In 1934, at the height of his popularity, Buck filmed *The Fighting Ranger*. A remake of *Border Law*, Buck once more played a Ranger given a leave of absence to track down his brother's killer. A rising actor in a feature role was young Ward Bond, who in 1956 would play a Ranger captain in one of the best Westerns ever filmed.

Ken Maynard also remade *Border Law*, as *Whistlin' Dan* in 1932. Another 1932 Ranger film was *Come On Danger!*, starring Tom Keene as a Ranger in pursuit of his brother's killer. There is another female Robin Hood; the outlaw hideout is in

Buck Jones apprehending a villain. At the height of his popularity during the 1930s, Buck embraced Texas Ranger roles, and his fan club was named the Buck Jones Rangers.

Hidden Valley; and Keene trounces the gang leader in a climactic fistfight. In future years *Come On Danger!* would be remade by O'Brien, Tim Holt, and Tex Ritter.

There were two other Ranger films in 1932. *Texas Tornado* featured Lane Chandler as a 1930s Ranger battling gangsters who used Tommy guns to rustle cattle. In *Without Honor*, longtime Western star Harry Carey is a black-clad gambler-gunman who joins the Texas Rangers in order to prove that his murdered brother is innocent of various crimes. When handed his brother's badge, Carey drawls, "That's sure funny. Looks like

B Westerns

Most of the "oaters" or "horse operas" of the 1930s were B Westerns, films which formed the staple of the motion picture industry for decades. In Hollywood there were eight major studios which filmed A movies, features that were eighty to ninety minutes in length (and sometimes longer). B movies were shorter features, about fifty-five to sixty minutes, and were used for double bills. An A film would provide the feature attraction for a double bill, while the lower half was filled by a B movie (although sometimes a double bill was made up of two B features). Major studios maintained B units to produce Westerns, mysteries, serials and other short features, while a number of small "independent" studios concentrated their total efforts on B movies.

Although there were few A Westerns during the 1930s, hundreds of B Westerns were filmed. A star such as Ken Maynard, Buck Jones, or Gene Autry would sign a contract to produce a series of six to eight Westerns per year. A new Gene Autry movie, therefore, would be released every month or two. By using the same actors, director, producer, crew, and even locations, a great deal of money and time could be saved on each film. A series would be modestly budgeted, at perhaps $8,000 to $12,000 per film, with around five days devoted to actual filming. B Westerns could be expected to earn at least $50,000, which provided solid profits with minimal investment for the studio.

The star, usually wearing a big white hat and riding a fine horse (with a name), was immediately identifiable as the hero, but the villains were equally identifiable. The character actors who played bad guys appeared in one Western after another; fans might not know their names, but their scowling faces were instantly recognized—and they usually wore black hats. There was a lot of action, and within an hour the star defeated the villains and justice had triumphed.

This formula remained popular with young fans through the 1940s and into the 1950s, even though Westerns increasingly were filmed as A productions with major stars. Because of the sheer numbers of B Westerns, therefore, the majority of Ranger movies were series films.

the law's got me at last." One of the actors is George Hayes, who was gradually developing the "Gabby" persona that would make him the best sidekick in the business.

George Hayes was a comic bad guy the next year in *The Ranger's Code*. Bob Steele, directed by his father, starred as a Texas Ranger torn between arresting or releasing his sweetheart's brother. Bob releases the suspect, then works to prove him innocent.

In 1933 Bob Steele starred in The Ranger's Code, *the same year that he played an Arizona Ranger in* Trailin' North. *A boyhood friend of John Wayne, in 1960 Bob appeared in Duke's Texas Ranger movie,* The Comancheros.

A far more important Ranger entertainment began in 1933. The most famous fictional Ranger of all time was introduced on network radio, before being brought to movie screens and to television. Technical developments early in the 1920s made possible the mass manufacture of radios and an explosion of stations, from 80 to more than 600, a number that continued to grow every year. In 1926 NBC created the first radio network, and others soon followed. The networks competed fiercely for popular singers and other stars, and there was an insatiable demand for programming, including dramas, comedies—and Westerns.

The Lone Ranger was the creation of George W. Trendle. The initial broadcast of *The Lone Ranger* emanated from Detroit's WXYZ on January 31, 1933. The juvenile western show won immediate popularity and within a year it was the cornerstone of a new radio network, the Mutual Broadcasting System. The thirty-minute program aired at 7:30 three nights a week. And on each of these three evenings, there were three live performances, to accommodate the three time zones.

The initial episode, which was repeated on a regular basis through the years, centered around the ambush of a band of Texas Rangers by the Butch Cavandish Gang. The six Rangers were led by Captain Dan Reid, whose small command included his younger brother, John. The Reid brothers were partners in a rich silver mine, but they intended to stay with the Rangers until the notorious Cavendish Gang was apprehended. But they were guided into a deadly ambush in Bryant's Gap by their treacherous scout. Although the Rangers fought bravely, they were gunned down one by one. Captain Reid asked John to provide his wife and son Danny with income from the silver mine. (George Trendle soon created an-

other popular program, *The Green Hornet*. A modern crime fighter, The Green Hornet was a secret identity of crusading newspaperman, Britt Reid, son of Dan Reid—and great nephew of the Lone Ranger!)

When John Reid fell wounded beside his dead brother, all six Rangers lay still on the canyon floor, and the outlaws rode away. That night, under a bright moon, the fallen Rangers were discovered by an Indian. Finding that John Reid was still alive, the Indian carried the injured Ranger to a cave and tended his wounds. Then the Indian buried the five dead Rangers, creating a sixth grave so that outlaws would not suspect there was a survivor.

After John Reid recovered consciousness four days later, he recognized his nurse as Tonto, a boyhood friend whose life he once saved. Reid would call Tonto "kemo sabe" ("faithful friend"). "You only Ranger left," Tonto informed Reid. "You Lone Ranger."

Reid announced his intention to devote his life to the battle for justice, and Tonto vowed to stay by his side. Reid devised a mask to conceal his identity. He employed a retired Texas Ranger, Jim Blaine, to work the silver mine, providing the Lone Ranger with income and silver bullets. When he acquired a magnificent white stallion, Tonto remarked, "Him shine like silver."

"Silver!" exclaimed the Lone Ranger. "That would be a great name for him." Silver would save the life of the Lone Ranger on many future occasions.

The Lone Ranger and Tonto soon captured the Cavendish Gang. When a later episode saw Butch escape from prison, the Lone Ranger tracked him to Bryant's Gap and killed him. But Butch Cavendish was the only man the Lone Ranger ever

would kill. He apprehended countless villains, but whenever shooting was necessary, the Lone Ranger always wounded his opponent. In addition to being an expert marksman and a superb fist-fighter, he was a master of disguise. He never drank or smoked, and spoke flawless grammar. Parents were delighted with such an exemplary role model.

"A fiery horse with the speed of light, a cloud of dust and a hearty Hi-Yo Silver! The Lone Ranger rides again!" Excited audiences listened expectantly for this introductory announcement accompanied by the swelling orchestral strains of *The William Tell Overture*. The Lone Ranger was first played by George Steinus, who soon was replaced by Earl Graser. John Todd played Tonto.

The show was written by the prolific Fran Striker, who had to churn out 156 Lone Ranger radio scripts a year in addition to his work on *The Green Hornet* and other shows! Soon Striker, who sometimes was aided by other writers, also was creating Lone Ranger comic books and comic strips, along with a dozen Lone Ranger novels. Then he would be called upon to write two fifteen-chapter Lone Ranger movie serials.

While *The Lone Ranger* captivated radio audiences, movie studios continued to serve up Ranger films. In 1935, for example, *Rough Riding Ranger* featured the exploits of Rex Lease and Yakima Canutt. Yak was a former rodeo champion who often played a bad guy while doubling the star as stunt man. During the 1930s Yak brought screen fights to realistic new levels, and he worked out one sensational stunt after another.

The next year was celebrated as the centennial of Texas history—1936 had been the year of the Alamo, the Texas Declaration of Independence, San Jacinto, and the beginning

of the Lone Star Republic. The Texas Centennial of 1936 generated numerous Texas Ranger movies.

The most recent Western star was a native Texan, Gene Autry, who had created a sensation as a singing cowboy. Gene's twelfth movie, *Ride, Ranger, Ride*, was released on September 30, 1936. In this film the Ranger role in battling Comanches is emphasized. Texas has just been admitted to the Union (1846, although costumes and weapons belong to a later period), and the Rangers have been disbanded, turning their Indian fighting duties over to the U.S. Cavalry. *Ride, Ranger, Ride* opens with Ranger Lt. Autry riding at the head of his recently disbanded company. Lt. Autry leads his men singing the title song ("You're a loyal Texas son/And she needs you every one"). When the song ends, Gene announces that he has received a lieutenant's commission in the Cavalry. Gene's sidekick, Smiley Burnette, persuades the entire company to enlist under their former leader at "Fort Adobe."

At the fort an "Admission Day Celebration" features the music of "Gene Autry and His Rangers." Following the concert Gene and his horse, Champion, win a race as his men chant, "Ride, Ranger, ride!" Gene falls in love with the daughter of Fort Adobe's colonel. But the colonel objects to Gene's aggressive tactics against Comanches and demands his resignation. Now out of the army (along with Smiley and his men, who somehow have left their enlistments), Gene persuades the governor to reinstate the Rangers. Soon Lt. Autry and his men ride to the rescue of a wagon train under attack by Comanches, who finally are routed by the U.S. Cavalry. In the closing scene Gene marries the colonel's daughter. Gene and his bride—both dressed in gleaming white—march beneath an arch of upheld weapons: drawn sabers by a line of cavalry-

Gene Autry in a costume worn as Ranger Lt. Autry in Ride, Ranger, Ride.

men, and carbines by Texas Rangers. As the happy couple head toward their honeymoon in a horse-drawn carriage, there is a final chorus of "Ride, Ranger, Ride."

Gene promptly launched his next film, *The Big Show*, which would include real Texas Rangers. "The Big Show" was the Texas Centennial Exposition held at the State Fairgrounds in Dallas. The film crew traveled to Dallas, and in the future location shooting frequently would enhance Autry movies. In *The Big Show* Gene played dual roles: an unlikable cowboy movie star named Tom Ford, and his look-alike stunt double—Gene Autry. Indeed, there is a fine scene of Western movie-making at Republic Studios in the 1930s. After his movie wraps, Tom Ford immediately leaves for a remote vacation, unaware that the studio's publicist has booked him for an appearance at the Texas Centennial Exposition.

The publicist persuades a reluctant Gene Autry to impersonate Ford in Dallas. The new buildings erected at the State Fairgrounds for the 1936 Exposition are shown, along with the Southern Methodist University marching band and about forty "Texas Rangers," marching in formation and singing—what else?—*Ride, Ranger, Ride*. A representative of the governor of Texas presents Gene with a Texas Ranger commission and introduces him to towering Ranger "Captain Leonard Pack "and his famous horse Texas." (Pack actually was a career lawman who served as a Special Texas Ranger from 1933-1935.) At the Exposition Gene performs and sings with the Light Crust Doughboys, The Beverly Hill Billies, and the Sons of the Pioneers. (The Pioneers, which included Len Slye—soon to be cowboy star Roy Rogers—were playing a lengthy gig at the Dallas Exposition, and were launching a movie career that would include more than 100 films.) A subplot involved gang-

sters who were chased down by Gene and the Rangers. Because of the singing ability he exhibited, Gene returns to Hollywood as the first singing cowboy—with Tom Ford as his double.

The song *Ride, Ranger, Ride* had been written by Tim Spencer, a member of the fast-rising Sons of the Pioneers. The lyrics include: "You have conquered every foe/Since a hundred years ago." The noted University of Texas professor of history, Dr. Walter Prescott Webb, published a landmark Ranger study, *The Texas Rangers*, in 1935. Webb intended his book to be a centennial history, contending that the Rangers had been founded in 1835. In recent years some historians have suggested that Rangers may have ridden as early as 1823. But during the 1936 Texas Centennial it was felt that the Rangers were beginning their second century, operating under the newly organized Department of Public Safety.

With attention drawn to the century-old Rangers by Webb's book and the long Texas Centennial celebration, Paramount Pictures decided to film a feature-length Western entitled *The Texas Rangers*. In charge of the project was a native Texan, King Vidor, one of Hollywood's top directors. Vidor produced, directed, and helped write *The Texas Rangers*. According to the opening credits, the screenplay was "Based Upon Data Furnished By Walter Prescott Webb's Book, *The Texas Rangers*," but any connections to the Webb study were scant. At least the film was dedicated to the Texas Rangers. King Vidor tried to sign Gary Cooper, but he had to settle for Fred MacMurray. Other cast members included Jack Oakie, Lloyd Nolan, Jean Parker, and George Hayes as a judge.

Released in 1936, *The Texas Rangers* ran for an hour and thirty-five minutes in black and white. MacMurray, Oakie and

Nolan are stagecoach robbers who are separated while escaping a posse. While Nolan follows an outlaw's life, MacMurray and Oakie join Company D of the Frontier Battalion of Texas Rangers. The Rangers battle Comanches, and MacMurray falls in love with his commander's daughter.

When MacMurray is sent to clean up a town, he is met at the train by leading citizens who are alarmed that there is only one Ranger. "Only one fight, ain't there?" replies MacMurray in a paraphrase of the famous One Riot One Ranger line. He quickly conquers the local villain, Jess Higgins, who has killed the two Hartford brothers. (Rangers of the Frontier Battalion broke up the Lampasas County feud between Pink Higgins, who had a rider named Jess Standard, and the Horrell brothers.) In the meantime, Nolan has created a crime wave across Texas. After he treacherously murders Oakie, MacMurray tracks him down and kills him.

Lloyd Nolan was a cheerfully evil villain. But as a Westerner Fred MacMurray was no Gary Cooper. Jack Oakie, as comic relief, was silly, and as MacMurray's sweetheart Jean Parker was decidedly unpretty. The script often was unbelievable, and so were many of the action sequences. But the timing was right for a slam-bang Ranger movie. *The Texas Rangers* was a box-office success, spawning a 1940 sequel, *Texas Rangers Ride Again*, and a 1949 remake, *Streets of Laredo*.

There were other Ranger movies in 1936. Bob Steele, again directed by his father, filmed *The Kid Ranger*. While tracking an outlaw gang, Ranger Bob shoots an innocent man, then vows to bring Texas justice to the real bad guys. In *Fast Bullets* Tom Tyler starred as a veteran Ranger in 1930s Texas, aided by young Ranger Rex Lease. The Rangers struggled with racketeers on the range, a favorite storyline in Westerns of the

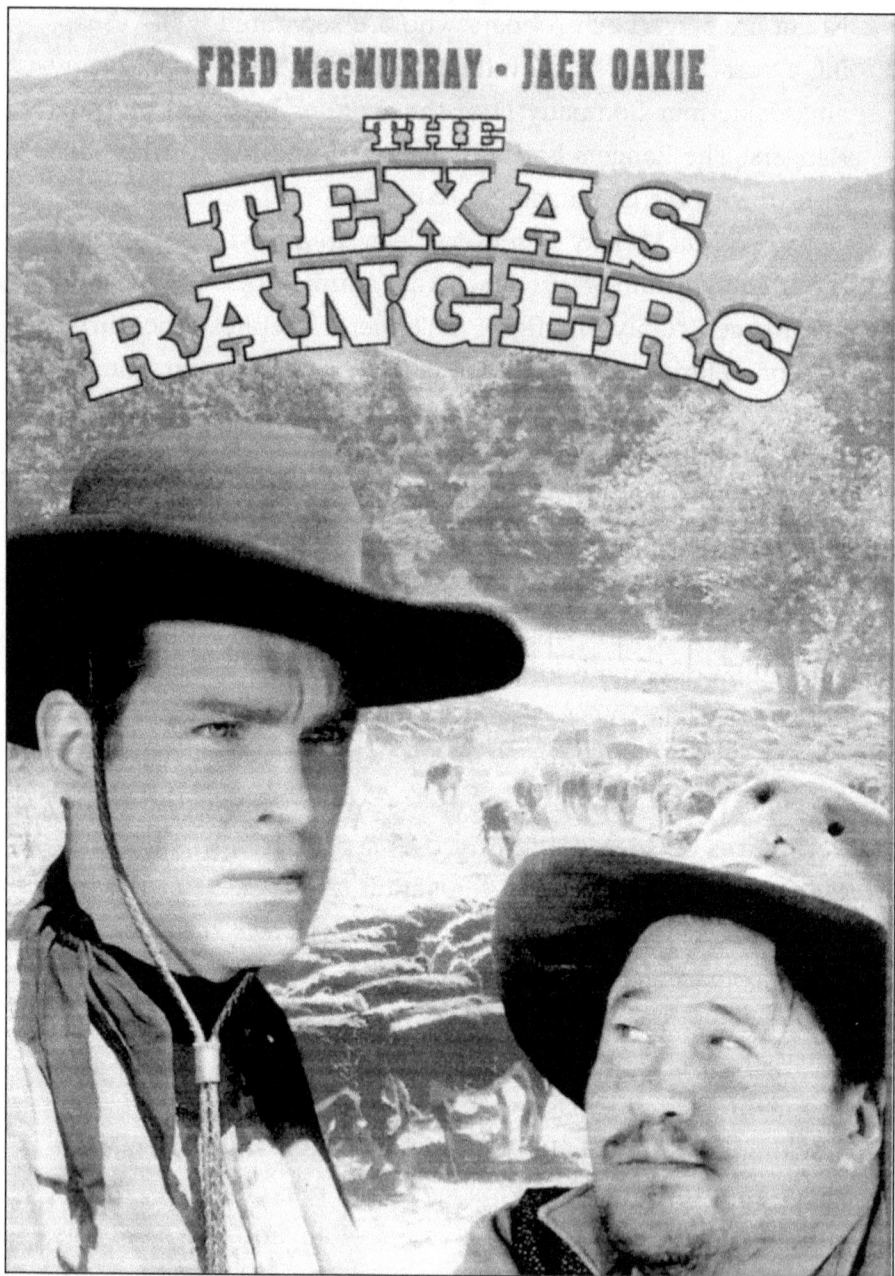

The Texas Rangers *was released during the Texas Centennial, 1936, and was remade 13 years later.*

1930s (because of the great popularity of gangster movies during the decade). At one point during *Fast Bullets*, Rangers fool the dude gangsters by mounting dummies on horseback to decoy the outlaws.

Also in 1936 Columbia Pictures launched a six-film Texas Ranger series, starring Bob Allen. As Irvine Theodore Baehr, he was a standout athlete at Dartmouth in 1926 when he was given a bit part in *The Quarterback*, which was filmed on campus. (Dartmouth footballer Charles Starrett also began his career in *The Quarterback*.) Baehr soon changed his name to Bob Allen and acted in a variety of roles on Broadway and in Hollywood. After playing second lead in a few Tim McCoy Westerns, Columbia chose him to star in their new Texas Ranger series.

The first two films were released in 1936, while the others hit the screens the next year. "Ranger" was used in each of the six titles: *The Unknown Ranger, Rio Grande Ranger, Ranger Courage, Law of the Ranger, Reckless Ranger,* and *The Rangers Step In.* Although Allen's acting background was a strong point, the Ranger films were routine and generally lackluster. Perhaps the best was *The Reckless Ranger.* Bob's twin brother, a sheepman, is murdered by cattleman Harry Woods. Bob and fellow Ranger Jack Perrin (who once starred in his own Westerns), take on the bad guys, including veteran villain Bud Osborne.

But by 1937 Columbia's Western department was headlined by Buck Jones, and the studio was developing Charles Starrett as a cowboy star. Columbia dropped Bob Allen and his series. Bob tried to land a series at Republic, the best studio for B-Westerns, but contract player Len Slye was promoted to star in the series under the name Roy Rogers. Bob Allen soon

returned to New York, working on stage and television during the remainder of his long career.

Meanwhile, Allen's Dartmouth teammate, Charles Starrett, became a top Western star. From 1935 through 1952, Starrett made 131 Westerns for Columbia. His second starring film,

Memorial Hall

While Texas celebrated its Centennial during 1936, a handsome two-story building was erected on the eastern edge of San Antonio's Brackenridge Park. Memorial Hall, with most of the second floor devoted to a large assembly hall, hosted well-attended reunion meetings of the Former Texas Rangers Association and the Old Trail Drivers Association. The structure was formally christened The Pioneers, Trail Drivers, and Texas Rangers Building, but often shortened to Pioneer Hall or Memorial Hall.

Many of the old lawmen and pioneer cattlemen donated historical artifacts, which were displayed in cases. In 1972 the building was officially designated a museum, although meetings still were held in the upstairs assembly hall. While the Ranger collection is far less extensive than the vast array of items at the Texas Ranger Hall of Fame and Museum in Waco, San Antonio's Ranger museum is well worth a visit.

Beginning in 1936, Charles Starrett starred as a Texas Ranger in 15 movies, more than any other actor.

The Mysterious Avenger, was released in 1936. Starrett is a Texas Ranger whose rancher father is accused of rustling by the real villain.

The next year Starrett again played a Ranger in one of his best films, *Outlaws of the Prairie*. The Sons of the Pioneers, now without Roy Rogers, had become regulars in Starrett movies. In the era of the singing cowboys, Starrett could not sing, so the Pioneers provided several songs per film. *Tumbling Tumbleweeds*, written by Bob Nolan, was the theme song of the Starrett-Pioneer movies. The Pioneers made thirty films with Starrett, and Bob Nolan usually played second lead. In *Outlaws of the Prairie* Starrett and the Pioneers comprised a Texas Ranger squad, with considerable singing in camp or at the "Tres Nogales Ranger Station." During a grisly piece of villainy, the bad guys cut off Starrett's trigger finger. But the big hero began wearing gloves and fanning his revolver, and thereby was able to take on the bad guys again. Starrett would return to Ranger roles in the 1940s.

Another former football star, Johnny Mack Brown, also became a longtime cowboy hero who occasionally played a Texas Ranger. An All-American back from Alabama in 1927, Brown played in the Rose Bowl in 1926 and 1927, and he soon returned to California. He was a Western star throughout the 1930s and 1940s and into the 1950s. In 1937 Brown was a Texas Ranger in *Lawless Land*, investigating a series of killings.

Also in 1937 Kermit Maynard, brother of Ken, played a Texas Ranger trying to foil a crook who is trying to buy ranch land cheap before word of a gold discovery leaks out. (Texas, of course, was not famous for its gold discoveries.) Bob Steele made another Ranger movie in 1937, directed as usual by his

father. *The Gun Ranger* is set in 1930s Texas. When a judge lets a murderer go free, Bob throws down his Ranger badge and rides to impose gun justice.

In 1938 Colonel Tim McCoy made two Ranger movies. McCoy was a Wyoming rancher who rose to the rank of lieutenant colonel during World War I (returning to the service in World War II, he was a colonel who won the Bronze Star for combat in Europe). McCoy starred in silent films, then easily made the transition to talkies. Clad in black, he sported a tall hat and a flowing white bandana. *Code of the Rangers* was set in the 1930s, but Tim and his fellow Rangers rode horseback. They wore the famous wagon wheel badges. Tim discovers that his Ranger brother, Rex Lease, is a secret member of an outlaw gang. After he goes to prison in place of his younger brother, Tim receives a governor's pardon through the efforts of his sweetheart. Immediately reinstated as a Ranger (!), Sgt. McCoy goes after the gang. His brother redeems himself by taking a bullet meant for Tim, who then finishes off the bad guys. Also in 1938, Tim made *The Phantom Ranger*. He pretends to be an outlaw in order to corral a band of counterfeiters.

Another 1938 release was *Man's Country*, starring Jack Randall and lovely Marjorie Reynolds. Randall is a Ranger chasing a gang whose leader was a twin brother. Randall's brother in real life was cowboy hero Bob Livingston, who soon would play the Lone Ranger. During World War II Randall enlisted in the Army Air Corps, rising to the rank of captain. Tragically, upon his return to film work in 1945, he was killed when a galloping horse ran him into a tree.

Fred Scott, "The Silvery Voiced Buckaroo," interrupted an operatic career for a brief run as a singing cowboy. In *The*

Col. Tim McCoy, a veteran of both World Wars, played Sgt. Tim Strong in Code of the Rangers *(1938).*

Ranger's Roundup, a 1938 release, Fred is a Texas Ranger in pursuit of bad guys operating out of a traveling medicine show. Ranger Fred finds time during the fifty-five minute film to croon five tunes.

A far more enduring singing cowboy began starring in Westerns in 1938. After Len Slye left the Sons of the Pioneers to sign a contract with Republic Studios, he played small parts in a couple of films as Dick Weston. Then, early in 1938, Republic's star singing cowboy, Gene Autry, went on strike just before beginning a new film. Republic rushed Len Slye/Dick Weston into the role, changing his name again to Roy Rogers (reminiscent of the beloved Will Rogers). Although Gene Autry settled his contractual problems with Republic, Roy Rogers continued to star in his own films.

The third Roy Rogers movie was *Come On, Ranger*, with a similar storyline to Republic's 1936 Gene Autry film, *Ride Ranger, Ride*. With Texas now a state, the governor decides to rely upon the protection of the U.S. Cavalry. Feeling that the state can no longer afford to maintain the Rangers, he decides to disband the force. When Ranger Captain Roy Rogers informs his men that they have been terminated by the governor, one Ranger shouts prophetically: "Doesn't he know he's terminating law and order in Texas?"

Roy's older brother and fellow Ranger, Lane Chandler, returns to his ranch and his wife. Roy and sidekick Raymond Hatton (Roy would later team with the best of all sidekicks, Gabby Hayes) ride to Fort Kendall to join the cavalry. Roy is soon promoted to sergeant, and he competes with an officer played by Lee Powell for the affections of the colonel's daughter, pretty Mary Hart. (When Lynne Roberts was cast in the film, the studio insisted that she change her name, so that

In Come On, Rangers, *only his third starring role, young Roy Rogers played a Ranger captain.*

Republic could have its own version of Broadway's "Rogers and Hart." Roy Rogers and Mary Hart teamed as a romantic duo in seven films, but his most famous co-star would be Dale Evans).

"OUTLAWS POUR INTO TEXAS!" proclaim newspaper headlines. When Roy's brother and sister-in-law are killed in a raid on their ranch, he deserts the cavalry to go after the gang. After Roy publicly challenges the gang leader, one citizen announces, "I'll take a Ranger's word against anybody!" Rounding up his old Ranger company, Roy destroys the outlaw gang. The governor reinstates the Texas Rangers, and Roy is dismissed from the cavalry to once again pin on his Ranger badge (a simple star). With more than eighty movies ahead of him, Roy again would take up a Ranger role.

The most important Ranger film of 1938 was *The Lone Ranger*. For five years *The Lone Ranger* had generated swelling popularity among radio audiences, while Lone Ranger comic books and other spinoffs made a movie version inevitable. Republic Studios acquired film rights, and it was decided to bring the Lone Ranger to movie screens in a weekly serial. Two directors, John English and action expert William Witney, were assigned to the project.

From "Hi-Yo Silver!" to "The Last of the Rangers," fifteen chapters were filmed, totaling 264 minutes of screen time. Each chapter averaged seventeen or eighteen minutes, beginning with the ambush of a band of Rangers by outlaws. The lone survivor, Alan King (not John Reid, for some reason), is taken to a cavern and nursed back to health by an Indian named Tonto. "Other Rangers all dead," said Tonto to his patient. "You only man Tonto find alive."

"The only one. The Lone Ranger," mused King, fondling

his badge (a star with "RANGER" engraved across the middle). "I'll never rest until these deaths are avenged."

While avenging those deaths, the Lone Ranger rode a magnificent white horse, fired silver bullets, and disguised his identity with a black mask. Galloping across the Texas countryside he shouted "Hi-yo, Silver!," while Rossini's *William Tell Overture* throbbed along the soundtrack. In addition to Tonto, the Lone Ranger was aided by four stalwart men who dressed exactly as he did, including the same hat crease.

Since the Lone Ranger was never seen without his mask, movie audiences did not know which of the five identically-clad men was the central hero. But in later episodes, the five men began to be killed in action, one by one. As each man was slain, he was buried in the Lone Ranger's cavern hideout, until only the title hero was left alive. The Lone Ranger was asked to rejoin the Texas Rangers, but he preferred to remain a freelance operator against outlawry.

"If Texas ever needs me," declares the Lone Ranger before galloping away with Tonto, "I will return."

Lee Powell was selected by Republic as the first actor to portray the Lone Ranger onscreen. Powell never before had starred in a Western, and Republic apparently decided to cast a relative unknown so that it would not be obvious which of the five heroes was the Lone Ranger. The other four doomed heroes were played by Bruce Bennett (a better known actor than Powell and the last to be killed), Lane Chandler (who played a Ranger in *Come On, Ranger*, with Roy Rogers), young George Montgomery (who would star in *The Texas Rangers* in 1951), and Hal Taliaferro (who had been a star in earlier years). A priest friendly to the Lone Ranger was played by William Farnum (who had starred as Rangers in

In The Lone Ranger, *five masked men went after the bad guys. One by one they died in the line of duty, until only the Lone Ranger remained. There was a large supply of the black masks, because most stuntmen chewed tobacco.*

silent versions of *Riders of the Purple Sage* and *The Lone Star Ranger*).

The role of Tonto was created by big, rugged-looking Chief Thundercloud, a veteran stuntman and Wild West show performer from Oklahoma. For those accustomed only to Jay Silverheels as Tonto, Chief Thundercloud may offer a more formidable companion to the Lone Ranger.

For legions of young fans who may have tried to envision in mind's eye the radio adventures of the Lone Ranger, the serial provided thrilling visualization. It was a special experience to see the Lone Ranger and Silver and Tonto and even silver bullets. For fifteen weeks—usually each Saturday for nearly four months in 1938—youthful movie audiences were mesmerized by the adventures of the Lone Ranger.

Such profitable success dictated a sequel. *The Lone Ranger Rides Again* would be another fifteen-part serial, to be released early in 1939. Republic again assigned William Witney and John English as directors. Chief Thundercloud would return as Tonto, but the rest of the cast changed. (The Lone Ranger proved to be Powell's career high point; he joined the U.S. Marines in 1942 and was killed in action in the Pacific in 1945.)

For *The Lone Ranger Rides Again*, Republic would use an established Western star, along with the popular trio concept. In 1936 Republic launched a Three Mesquiteers series, a Western variant of the Three Musketeers. The series would last through 1943, with fifty-one Three Mesquiteers films. Handsome Bob Livingston created the character of Stoney Brooke, a role he played fifteen times by 1938. Livingston also played the masked rider Zorro in the 1937 Republic movie, *The Gay Cabellero*. Other studios created their own

The Lone Ranger Rides Again *was a 1939 sequel to* The Lone Ranger, *the 1938 serial which introduced the popular radio character to moviegoers.*

Western trios, including the Trail Blazers, the Rough Riders, and Range Busters—and the Texas Rangers.

Republic cast Bob Livingston as the Lone Ranger, and inserted Duncan Renaldo, who would soon join the Three Mesquiteers series. The Lone Ranger, Tonto, and Duncan Renaldo therefore would form a trio of heroes. One of the main villains was big Glenn Strange, a veteran bad guy who eventually would become respectable as Sam the Bartender on the long-running TV series *Gunsmoke*. One of the gang members was future singing cowboy Eddie Dean.

"I need another mask . . ."

On television and movie screens, Clayton Moore made the raccoon mask of the Lone Ranger famous. But the original celluloid Lone Ranger, in the 1938 and 1939 serials, covered the entire face. A stiff black mask concealed the upper half of his countenance, while a black net dropped down below the chin.

The many exciting feats enjoyed by Lone Ranger fans were performed by stunt men—who chewed tobacco. No one wanted to don a mask dripping with tobacco juice, so enough masks were stockpiled to equip anyone who might appear on-screen as the Lone Ranger.

In the opening credits of *The Lone Ranger Rides Again*, Bob Livingston is introduced as the title hero. From the first chapter, "The Lone Ranger Returns," there is non-stop action—fistfights, shootouts, and breakneck chases—as the hero trio battles the "Black Raiders." Livingston and Renaldo frequently hang out together in town picking up clues. Livingston rides a dark horse and wears a dark shirt. But when it is time for the Lone Ranger to ride, Livingston executes a quick change, in the manner of Clark Kent/Superman. Usually helped by Tonto, he pulls off his shirt—the Lone Ranger's shirt is worn underneath—and dons a mask and a hat and two-gun rig—then leaps onto Silver and gallops away to do good.

Although *The Lone Ranger Rides Again* pleased young fans, there would not be another Lone Ranger film until 1956. Furthermore, the negatives for both serials soon disappeared. *The Lone Ranger* was cut down to feature length in 1940 for *Hi-Yo Silver*, which is available today on video and provides a shortened version of the 1938 sequel. Eventually a print was discovered in Mexico of the 1939 sequel, so more than four hours of *The Lone Ranger Rides Again* may be viewed on video. Westerns were enormously popular in Mexico, and Republic regularly provided prints with Spanish subtitles to Mexican theaters. Since the word "tonto" means "fool or dunce" in Spanish, each time the Lone Ranger addressed his faithful companion by name onscreen, the subtitle read "Ponto" so that Mexican audiences would not laugh.

In 1939 a new series of seven Three Mesquiteers films was begun, starring Bob Livingston, Duncan Renaldo, and Raymond Hatton as the hero trio. The first of these movies, *Kansas Terrors*, was released by Republic while *The Lone*

Ranger Rides Again still played in theaters. It was not coincidental that during a scene in *Kansas Terrors* Bob Livingston appeared in his complete Lone Ranger outfit, including his mask and white horse.

Throughout the 1930s Hollywood regularly paraded Texas Rangers before moviegoers. Top Western stars portrayed Ranger heroes. An image was established of courageous Texas lawmen battling outlaw gangs and sometimes Comanche war parties. Rangers operated onscreen in fictional Texas towns and forts, and often they wore the wrong type of badge. But celluloid Rangers of the 1930s were fearless, resourceful men who were superb riders and deadly shots—a formidable portrait that audiences sensed was close to reality. And since these audiences were largely juvenile, they would grow up ready to enjoy more Ranger adventures in subsequent decades.

In Kansas Terrors, *a 1939 Three Mesquiteers movie, Robert Livingston dons the costume from his recent starring role in* The Lone Ranger Rides Again.

The 1930s

BEST WESTERN MOVIES
The Lone Ranger (1930—George O'Brien)
The Texas Ranger (1931—Buck Jones)
The Fighting Ranger (1934—Buck Jones)
Ride, Ranger, Ride (1936—Gene Autry)
The Texas Rangers (1936—Fred MacMurray)

BEST RANGER SERIAL
The Lone Ranger (1938—Lee Powell)

BEST RANGER RADIO PROGRAM
The Lone Ranger (1933—Earl Graser)

BEST RANGER BOOK
The Texas Rangers (1935—W. P. Webb)

BEST RANGER MAGAZINE SERIAL
"The Dude Ranger," McCall's (1930—Zane Grey)

RANGER EVENTS
- Budget slashes caused by the Depression limit the Ranger force to no more than 45 men during the 1930s.
- Future Captain M.T. "Lone Wolf" Gonzaullus tames the wild oil boomtown Kilgore (1930).
- After openly opposing Miriam A. Ferguson in the 1932 governor's race, all 44 Rangers are fired by Governor "Ma" Ferguson in January 1933. She then appoints 2,300 "special" Rangers.
- Former Ranger Captain Frank Hamer leads a successful manhunt for outlaws Bonnie and Clyde (1934).
- The Texas Rangers become part of the newly organized Department of Public Safety (1935).

1940s: Rangers, Rangers, Everywhere

"A Texas Ranger must shoot like a Tennessean, ride like a Mexican, and fight like the devil!"

—Republic Pictures ad for
Ranger movie *Beyond the Law*

Western movies enjoyed a heyday during the 1940s. Singing cowboys and other B-Western stars remained popular through most of the decade, while a growing public appetite for big budget frontier sagas brought top talent to the Western genre. Meanwhile, network radio continued to feature *The Lone Ranger*, and at the end of the decade television provided an exciting new venue for Ranger tales.

Numerous Ranger movies filled theater screens in 1940. The most ballyhooed Western of the year, Cecil B. DeMille's *North West Mounted Police*, starred the incomparable Gary Copper as Texas Ranger Dusty Rivers. Raised on a Montana ranch, Cooper was tall, lean, and an effortless rider. Registering understated power on film, Copper was a gifted, versatile actor who twice won Academy Awards for Best Actor. One of the greatest of all Western stars, his only Ranger role was in *North West Mounted Police*.

Cecil B. DeMille was a Hollywood legend with a taste for lavish melodrama. He had directed Westerns since the silent

era, and he scored a hit in 1936 with *The Plainsman*, starring Gary Cooper as Wild Bill Hickok. In 1939 DeMille directed another spectacular Western, *Union Pacific*, with Joel McCrea, Barbara Stanwyck, and Robert Preston (along with Chief Thundercloud, fresh from his Tonto roles). *Union Pacific* was a boxoffice blockbuster, so DeMille immediately turned to another Western. He filmed *North West Mounted Police* in Technicolor, partly to show off the red coats of the Mounties. He also filmed this "outdoor" epic mostly indoors; DeMille preferred shooting on controlled soundstages, which gave his Westerns a cramped look.

Ranger Cooper comes to Canada in 1885 in pursuit of a killer who has become the instigator of the Riel Rebellion, an actual Indian uprising. Mounties are trying to put down the rebellion, and Cooper works with his Canadian counterparts. Cooper and one of the Mounties, a sergeant played by Preston Foster, compete for the affections of beautiful Madeline Carroll. Her brother, another Redcoat played by handsome Robert Preston, is seduced by a sexy half-blood portrayed by Paulette Goddard. Preston's understandable preoccupation with Goddard leads to the massacre of several Mounties, and he later is killed in redemption. Added to all of this are other colorful characters and sub-plots. In the end Cooper kills his prey and, leaving Madeline Carroll with Preston Foster, rides back to Texas with the fugitive's corpse. *North West Mounted Police* is overwrought and a bit confusing, but Gary Cooper's convincing Western persona produced one of the most memorable of all Ranger characterizations.

Roy Rogers made another Ranger film in 1940. During his early period as a cowboy star, Roy's movies were set in the historical West, and he played Billy the Kid, Wild Bill Hickok,

Gary Cooper in his only role as a Texas Ranger, in Cecil B. DeMille's North West Mounted Police.

and Jesse James (twice). In *The Ranger and the Lady*, Republic of Texas President Sam Houston has traveled to Washington D.C., to try to achieve statehood. Back in Texas, President Houston's assistant imposes a ruinous tax for access to the Santa Fe Trail, which had a cutoff through the Texas Panhandle. The crooked assistant is opposed by Roy Rogers, dressed in buckskins as Ranger Captain Colt. Roy is assisted by Sgt. Gabby Hayes and Julie Bishop, daughter of a murdered Texas Ranger captain. At the film's climax President Houston (who never visited the Panhandle in real life) returns from Washington. Clad in top hat and cape, Sam Houston leaves his carriage to ride with Roy in the final shootout! After two years as a cowboy hero, Roy Rogers had become the Number Three Western star, and growing audiences viewed his Texas Ranger portrayals.

For the third year in a row there was a Lone Ranger film. In 1940 Republic edited their 1938 serial, *The Lone Ranger*, from 264 minutes to a 69-minute feature film, *Hi-Yo Silver*. Obviously, a great deal of action had to be cut from the original. Old-timer Raymond Hatton and child actor Dick Jones were added to the cast as a 1940 twosome. By telling a curious little boy what he knows about the Lone Ranger, Hatton provides narration that links together the greatly abbreviated story. But *The Lone Ranger* remained fresh in the memories of young fans, and *Hi-Yo Silver*, with more than two-thirds cut from the original, had only mediocre success at the boxoffice. Despite the continuing popularity of *The Lone Ranger* on radio, there would not be another Lone Ranger movie for more than a decade and a half.

In 1940 Paramount produced two films as follow-ups to their 1936 success, *The Texas Rangers*. For *Rangers of Fortune* a top director was assigned—Sam Wood, who in 1940 also di-

rected Thorton Wilder's *Our Town* and *Kitty Foyle*, starring
Ginger Rogers. Fred MacMurray, star of *The Texas Rangers*,
would headline *Rangers of Fortune* as a renegade army officer.
A hero trio was rounded out by Gilbert Roland and Albert
Dekker. Discovering a Texas town overrun by hoodlums who
kill an elderly newspaperman—and his granddaughter—the
"Rangers of Fortune" clean out the bad guys. But the expected
trio series did not materialize from this routine film.

Paramount tried again with *Texas Rangers Ride Again*, an
announced sequel to *The Texas Rangers*. Set in the Texas of
1940, *Texas Rangers Ride Again* featured bland John Howard
and burly Broderick Crawford as undercover Rangers battling
rustlers. During the movie's preview, a bold sign flashed over
scenes from the film: "For 114 Years, the Texas Rangers Have
Carried on a Tradition of Courage and Glory!" A narrator then
proclaimed: "And now the Texas Rangers ride again. Combining
the knowledge of a modern scientist of crime with the fearless-
ness of the old-time frontier scout in this new age of speed."

Texas Rangers Ride Again, therefore, dealt with the transition the Rangers of 1940 were undergoing. The officers in
Texas Rangers Ride Again use short wave radios and drive
black Fords with "TEXAS RANGERS" painted on the doors.
But the Fords pull horse trailers—which frequently occurred in
1940—and the Rangers often gallop into the countryside.
There was a scene in Austin, showing the state capitol and
Ranger headquarters at Camp Mabry. Although the rustlers
rode horses and fired six-guns, they also utilized short wave
radios and trucks.

Their modern methods worked extremely well; one Texas
ranch owner stated that "a quarter million of our cattle" had
been stolen during the past year. This great ranch, the "White

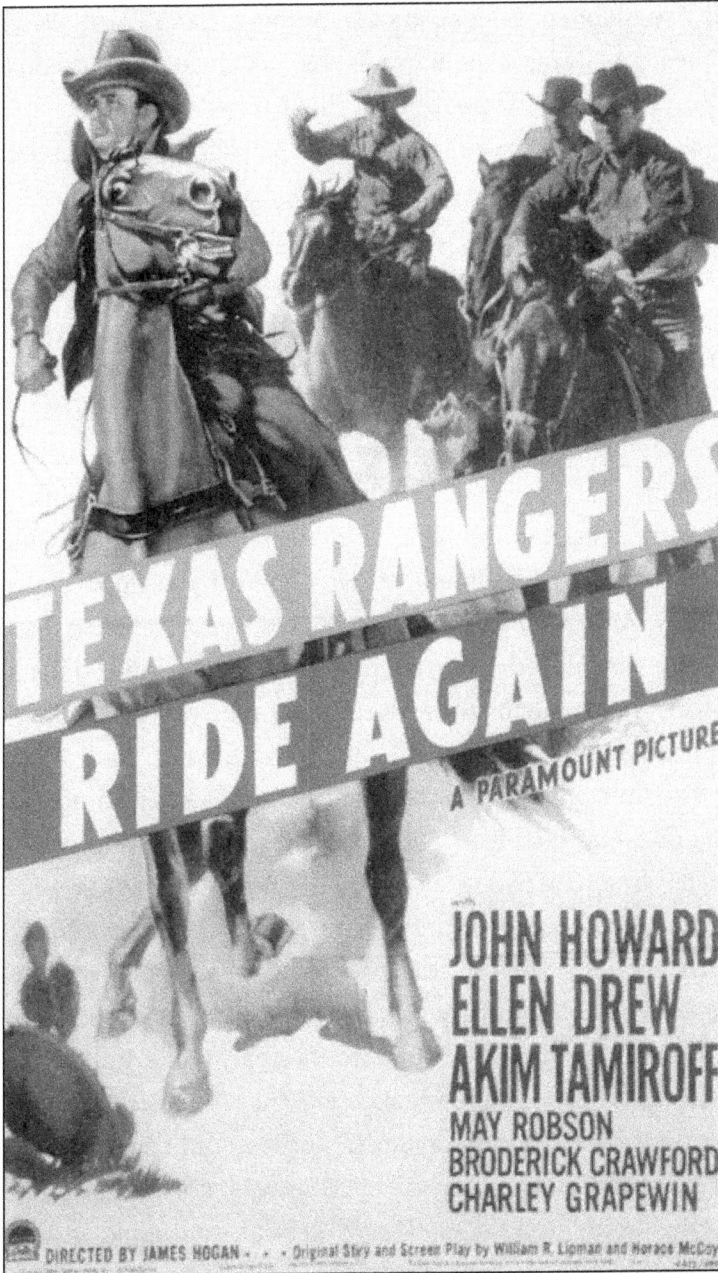

Texas Rangers Ride Again *was a lame sequel to the 1936 film,* The Texas Rangers.

Sage," employed 500 cowboys. (Only a handful of Western ranches ever ranged as many as 100,000 cattle or used 100 cowboys.) Most of the action on this "Texas" ranch takes place among Arizona's saguaro cactus. At one point Broderick Crawford shot the gun out of a bad guy's hand, just like the Lone Ranger or Ranger Charles Starrett.

Broderick Crawford was far more believable as a Ranger than Howard (Crawford would win the 1949 Academy Award for Best Actor for *All the King's Men*). At one point Crawford tossed his Ranger badge with a message to a surprised Robert Ryan. Ryan was unbilled, but he was excellent in his single scene, an indication that he would rise to stardom. Anthony Quinn was outstanding as a range boss who secretly leads the rustlers. Character actor Akim Tamiroff, who had a more important role in *North West Mounted Police*, provided comic relief. A Ranger captain was played by William Farnum, who had starred in Ranger roles in silent films. Ellen Drew received star billing opposite the ineffective Howard. But their romance and the comedy attempts were silly and unbelievable. Despite an able cast, *Texas Rangers Ride Again* was a hackneyed disappointment.

The first Charles Starrett film of 1940 was *Two-Fisted Rangers*. Once again, Starrett, pursuing the murderer of his sheriff brother, and the Sons of the Pioneers portrayed Texas Rangers. Iris Meredith, who co-starred with Starrett in eighteen films, provided the romantic interest, while hulking Dick Curtis, another Starrett regular, led the villains. Pioneer Bob Nolan ran for the vacated sheriff's office, and campaign music was provided by the Sons of the Pioneers.

The steady stream of Ranger movies continued in 1941. Twentieth Century Fox decided to lense a fourth version of Zane Grey's *Riders of the Purple Sage*. George Montgomery, a

featured actor in *The Lone Ranger* serial, starred as Jim Lassiter, the Texas Ranger on a manhunt that takes him to Utah. George Letz was raised on a Montana ranch and began film work as a stuntman. As his star rose he changed his last name to Montgomery, and he would play a succession of Ranger roles. Although released as a 56-minute B Western, *Riders of the Purple Sage* was a surprise success, partially due to the power of Grey's story and to the heroic qualities of the young, handsome Montgomery.

Fox pursued their past pattern by immediately following *Riders* with a Zane Grey sequel. Montgomery was cast as Buck Duane in the fourth version of *Last of the Duanes*. Lynne Roberts, who had been in *The Lone Ranger*, *Come On Rangers* (as "Mary Hart" opposite Roy Rogers), and *Riders of the Purple Sage*, played a heroine. One of the bad guys was Lane Chandler, who was a Ranger good guy in *The Lone Ranger* and *The Lone Ranger Rides Again*. And playing Major McNeil of the Texas Rangers was William Farnum, who had played the lead in the first version of *Riders of the Purple Sage* (1918) and *The Lone Star Ranger* (1919).

Texas Rangers are prominent in the 1941 version of *Last of the Duanes*. Major McNeil and a company of Rangers are encamped near Huntsville, and there is a scene at the Ranger headquarters fort (which never existed). The Rangers wear a wagon wheel badge and a uniform topped with a Smokey the Bear hat. (Rangers never had a uniform, but in *Last of the Duanes* they look like modern members of the National Park Service.) Buck Duane rescues a friend from Ranger custody, then later agrees to work undercover with the Rangers against a bandit gang operating along the Mexican border. Eve Arden plays an outlaw lady who falls in love with Buck Duane, and who takes a bullet

fired at him by the outlaw leader. That leader—a Ranger captain gone bad—is promptly shot by Buck. In the final scene Major McNeil pins a Ranger badge on Buck Duane.

One of the 1941 B Westerns about Rangers starred Don "Red" Barry. A native Texan, Barry was short of stature, but radiated an explosive personality, and he was regarded as the Jimmy Cagney of Westerns. He was nicknamed "Red" after Republic starred him in a 1940 serial about comic strip hero Red Ryder. Republic gave him the lead in twenty-nine Westerns, including *Desert Bandit*, in which Barry was a Texas Ranger tracking gun smugglers along the Rio Grande. Lynn Merrick, Barry's leading lady in more than half of his films, graced *Desert Bandit*, and veteran villain Charles King provided opposition. King was from Hillsboro, Texas, and in a long career as a bad guy, the heavyset Texan with a deep growl for a voice provided villainy in many Ranger films of the 1930s and 1940s.

In *Dynamite Canyon*, tall Tom Keene goes undercover to catch the murderer of a Texas Ranger and a rancher. Former football star Johnny Mack Brown made another Ranger movie in 1941, *Rawhide Ranger*. Ranger Brown goes in search of his brother's killer, soon riding into a town that is being terrorized by a criminal gang. It takes Ranger Brown less than an hour to clean out the bad guys. Another onetime football standout, Charles Starrett, starred as a Texas Ranger in *Riders of the Badlands*. Ranger Starrett is arrested because he looks like the villain, but he is helped out of trouble by a dentist, played by Russell Hayden.

An even greater football hero was Slingin' Sammy Baugh, a two-time All-American (1936 and 1937) for Texas Christian University. Baugh went from TCU to the NFL, where a stellar

Don "Red" Barry, the "Jimmy Cagney of Westerns," starred as a Ranger in Desert Bandit.

career eventually earned him election to the Pro Football Hall of Fame. By 1941 he was an NFL sensation, the best passing quarterback the league had ever seen. Popular sports heroes such as Babe Ruth and Lou Gehrig had earlier been placed in the movies, and Republic signed Slingin' Sammy Baugh to star in *King of the Texas Rangers*.

The twelve-chapter serial was filmed in the summer of 1941, when Baugh had no football duties. The directors were William Witney and John English, who had directed *The Lone Ranger* and *The Lone Ranger Rides Again* in the late 1930s. In *The Lone Ranger Rides Again* Duncan Renaldo had ridden alongside the Lone Ranger, a role he would duplicate with Slingin' Sammy. Kermit Maynard also was in the cast, along with Iron Eyes Cody, former cowboy hero Buddy Roosevelt, and Roy Barcroft, Republic's "King of the Heavies," who played a villain in more than 200 films.

By 1941 Europe was in the second year of World War II, and Hollywood screenwriters began to work Nazi operatives into numerous films, especially Westerns. In *King of the Texas Rangers*, the first serial chapter is entitled, "The Fifth Column Strikes." Other chapter titles indicating contemporary Texas and the war situation included "Test Flight" and "Sky Raiders." Slingin' Sammy played Tom King, who gives up fame and fortune to join the Texas Rangers after his father is murdered. On the border Ranger King teams up with Duncan Renaldo, a Mexican officer trailing Axis spies.

The directors kept the action non-stop, and Witney always pushed the limits of violence for films aimed primarily for juvenile audiences. Indeed, the Hays Office—which existed to censor sex, profanity and violence from all motion pictures—heavily edited a number of the more violent scenes. In its final

form, the twelve chapters totaled 215 minutes, with the clos-ing segment endorsing the "Code of the Rangers." Slingin' Sammy happily returned to the gridiron, where his talents were unquestioned. Unlike Slingin' Sammy, *King of the Texas Rangers* re-emerged on movie screens, several years later, re-edited into six half-hour episodes (26½ minutes each, totaling 159 minutes).

Another Texan football star headlined *Lone Star Ranger* in 1942. The fourth version of Zane Grey's novel starred Jarrin' John Kimbrough, the All-American fullback who had led Texas A&M to the national championship in 1939. A fine actress, Sheila Ryan, was Jarrin' John's leading lady. William Farnum, who had starred in the first version in 1919, was a villainous land grabber. *Lone Star Ranger* was a mediocre film, and like Sammy Baugh, John Kimbrough left the field of acting to others.

Charles Starrett annually filmed seven or eight Westerns, and almost every year he included a Ranger movie. In 1942 his Ranger film was *Riders of the Northland*, the first B Western to deal with the condition that the United States was at war. Starrett and two other Texas Rangers are sent to Alaska to in-vestigate Nazi activities in the north. They discover that Nazi submarines are being secretly refueled, and that a runway for enemy planes is being constructed behind a barbed wire com-pound. The Rangers, of course, defeat the Nazi saboteurs.

For several years Columbia's two Western stars were Charles Starrett and "Wild Bill" Elliott. But in 1941 Columbia became interested in the trio concept popularized by the Three Mesquiteers. Tex Ritter was signed to co-star with Elliott in eight Westerns that also would feature a sidekick nicknamed "Cannonball." The last film in this series, *Vengeance of the West*, was released in 1942. Elliott plays a rancher whose fam-

ily has been murdered, while Ritter is "Ranger Captain Tex Lake."

Tim Holt made two Ranger movies in 1942. Holt filmed series Westerns for RKO from 1940 through 1952. One of his six starring films in 1942 was *Bandit Ranger*, and another was a remake of *Come On Danger*. RKO had first filmed *Come On Danger* in 1932 with Tom Keene. In the 1938 remake, *Renegade Ranger*, George O'Brien had the lead, young Rita Hayworth played a female Robin Hood, and Tim Holt and Ray Whitley had featured roles. In 1942 RKO dusted off the old script and placed Tim Holt in the lead, supported by Ray

In Vengeance of the West *(1942), Tex Ritter (kneeling) played "Ranger Captain Tex Lake."*

—Courtesy Texas Country Music Hall of Fame, Carthage

Whitley. In the most recent *Come On Danger*, Frances Neal hardly measured up to Rita Hayworth, but Tim Holt was superior to both Tom Keene and George O'Brien.

Late in 1942 the first film of a new series, "The Texas Rangers," was released by Producers Releasing Corporation. Organized in 1940, PRC was a small studio which filmed low-budget Westerns, mysteries, comedies, and musicals aimed at bobbysoxers. With "The Texas Rangers," PRC envisioned a series that would combine the trio concept, popularized by the Three Mesquiteers, with elements of the singing cowboy.

The trio would consist of a gunslinging lawyer, a Texas Ranger, and a comic sidekick. James Newill, a superb singer who had starred in a series as Renfrew of the Royal Mounted, was signed to play the lawyer. Dave "Tex" O'Brien, from San Angelo, would play Ranger Dave Wyatt. The handsome O'Brien wore a black outfit with a white hat and a long white neckerchief. Dave carried one six-gun and usually did not wear a Ranger badge, since he often worked undercover. The sidekick, Panhandle Perkins, was played by gangly Guy Wilkerson.

Each movie ran the following Foreword after the opening credits: "Dedicated to the law officers of the Old West, who led the fight for law and order in the pioneer days of this country in 1880." The first movie in the series, *The Rangers Take Over*, hit the screens late in 1942. Early the next year *Bad Men of Thunder Gap* was released, followed by six more films in 1943. There were nine Texas Rangers movies in 1944, followed by five more before the series ended in 1945. Over a period of nearly three years during World War II, "The Texas Rangers" appeared in a new film every six weeks.

The wavy-haired Newill did not cut much of a figure as a Western hero, and after fourteen Texas Rangers films he left

The Texas Ranger Series

From 1942 through 1945 "The Texas Rangers" was a series of twenty-two Westerns produced by PRC, a small studio which specialized in low-budget films. Dave "Tex" O'Brien was Ranger Dave Wyatt throughout the series, which also featured Tex Ritter, James Newill, and sidekick Guy Wilkerson.

1941	The Rangers Take Over
1943	Bad Men of Thunder Gap
	West of Texas
	Border Buckaroo
	Fighting Valley
	Trail of Terror
	Return of the Rangers
	Boss of Rawhide
1944	Gunsmoke Mesa
	Outlaw Roundup
	Guns of the Law
	The Pinto Bandit
	Spook Town
	Brand of the Devil
	Gangsters of the Frontier
	Dead or Alive
	The Whispering Skull
1945	Marked for Murder
	Enemy of the Law
	Three in the Saddle
	Frontier Fugitives
	Flaming Bullets

the movies to concentrate on his musical career. Newill's role was placed in the competent hands of Tex Ritter, who would play fast-shooting attorney "Tex Haines." Born on a Texas farm, Ritter had studied law for five years at the University of Texas before pursuing a show business career in New York City. Tex worked in Broadway shows and on network radio for several years. In 1936, because of the phenomenal success of Gene Autry, a talent scout came to New York in search of another singing cowboy. Tex Ritter owned a rich bass voice and a large portfolio of authentic cowboy songs which he had collected during his years in Austin. Over the next ten years he starred in sixty films and began a recording career that eventually placed him in Nashville's Country Music Hall of Fame. Tex rode a magnificent white stallion, White Flash, he excelled at fight scenes, and he regularly was voted among the Top Ten Western stars.

This established cowboy hero joined the Texas Rangers series in 1944, with *Gangsters of the Frontier*. Although a lawyer, he regularly helped Ranger Dave Wyatt chase the bad guys. Asked by a judge in *Dead or Alive* if he had his law books with him, Tex put his hands on his holstered six-guns: "Yep— both of 'em."

Tex headlined the last eight films of the Texas Rangers, ending with *Flaming Bullets* in 1945. *Flaming Bullets* also ended Tex Ritter's decade as a movie cowboy. Like James Newill, Ritter departed the Texas Rangers and concentrated upon his recording and performing career, which would include an eight-year television show.

During the war years movie theaters flourished across America. The Depression economy rebounded dramatically under war production, but the rationing of gasoline and tires

meant that entertainment had to be found close to home. Small farm communities boasted one or more downtown theaters, and rural audiences continued to demand Westerns. With Westerns still being produced by the hundreds, a significant number would be Ranger films.

In 1943, in addition to seven movies from the Texas Ranger series, Bob Steele was a Ranger in *Thundering Trails*, and Charles Starrett made *Hail to the Rangers*. Starrett played an ex-Ranger who comes to the aid of a rancher friend. A

Dave O'Brien (left), played Ranger Dave Wyatt in all 22 films of the "Texas Rangers" series, 1942-1945. Tex Ritter (right) co-starred in the last eight films. This still is from Enemy of the Law, *the nineteenth film of the series.*

—Courtesy Texas Country Music Hall of Fame, Carthage

strong cast included Arthur Hunnicut and young Lloyd Bridges.

Another young actor, big Robert Mitchum, began his remarkable career in 1943 with roles in nineteen movies. His first film was a Hopalong Cassidy Western, *Border Patrol*. In *Border Patrol* William Boyd, as Hoppy, played a Texas Ranger, along with his two sidekicks. Opposing the Rangers was a gang which included henchman Mitchum. Duncan Renaldo and George Reeves (TV's future Superman) also were in the cast.

Later in a busy year Mitchum appeared in another Ranger film, *Beyond the Last Frontier*. This movie was the first in a Republic series featuring a Texas Ranger character named John Paul Revere. Republic picked Eddie Dew, a bit player under contract, to play Ranger Revere. Smiley Burnette was cast as a Ranger, and, of course, Dew's sidekick. Robert Mitchum, in his fifteenth film of 1943, was Trigger Dolan, a swaggering bad guy.

"A Texas Ranger must shoot like a Tennessean, ride like a Mexican, and fight like the devil!" read Republic's advertising for *Beyond the Last Frontier*. But Eddie Dew, as John Paul Revere, hardly lived up to this Ranger job description. Dew was overshadowed by the screen presence of Robert Mitchum. Dew goes undercover to foil a band of gunrunners, reporting back to the Rangers, through Smiley Burnette. But the outlaw leader sends Mitchum to the Rangers as a spy. He is treated so well by the Rangers that he begins to rethink his career as a bad guy. Eventually Mitchum rescues Smiley from a burning barn, then helps the Rangers round up the gang. Mitchum is promised a Ranger commission after a short jail term.

Eddie Dew and *Beyond the Last Frontier* flopped with movie audiences. For the next film, *Raiders of Sunset Pass*,

John Paul Revere became a cowboy instead of a Ranger, but the result was another flop. Dew was dropped in favor of Robert Livingston, but after one more film—*Pride of the Plains*—the John Paul Revere series was cancelled.

In 1944 Charles Starrett's annual Ranger movie was *Cyclone Prairie Rangers*, who battled Nazis sabotaging cattle crops and farm equipment. Nine films from PRC's Texas Rangers series were released in 1944.

Starrett's 1945 Ranger film was *Both Barrels Blazing*, in which he plays a Texas Ranger clad in black costume and mask of the Durango Kid. The Ranger/Durango Kid goes after a villain who uses an old man as a front for stolen goods.

Future star Robert Mitchum (far right) made his screen debut in a 1943 Hopalong Cassidy movie, Border Patrol. *Hoppy (center) and his sidekicks played Texas Rangers.*

The Texas Rangers series ended in 1945 with the last five films. But also in 1945 the eighth film of Republic's Red Ryder series was *Lone Texas Ranger*. Republic had starred Don "Red" Barry in a 1940 serial based on the Red Ryder comic strip, and in 1944 they launched a series starring Wild Bill Elliott. Bobby Blake played Red Ryder's juvenile Indian sidekick, Little Beaver. Elliott would star in sixteen Red Ryder movies, and Allan "Rocky" Lane would succeed him in 1946. Lane made seven more Red Ryder films before the series ended in 1947.

In *Lone Texas Ranger*, Red Ryder is a Texas Ranger called upon to break up a crime wave in Silver City in 1896. The gang is led by two supposedly solid citizens: the town's famous sheriff, and a blacksmith played by the best villain in the business, Roy Barcroft. Ranger Ryder is forced to kill the sheriff after being fired upon, and finally he trounces Barcroft and the rest of the gang. Ranger Ryder's badge is a star encircled by the outline of a shield.

Charles Starrett, as the Durango Kid, starred in *Roaring Rangers* in 1946. The next year Starrett's Ranger film was *Riders of the Lone Star*. The Durango Kid and Smiley Burnette play Texas Rangers in search of a notorious outlaw. Also in 1947 singing cowboy Jimmy Wakely made a Ranger film, *Ridin' Down the Trail*. Wakely's sidekick was Dub Taylor, and Kermit Maynard and Charles King also were in the cast.

Jimmy Wakely and Dub Taylor were back in 1948 with *The Rangers Ride*. The same year Johnny Mack Brown, backed by Raymond Hatton, filmed *The Fighting Ranger*. A singing cowboy who was a far better singer than cowboy, Eddie Dean, made *The Tioga Kid* in 1948. A native Texan, Dean enjoyed considerable success as a radio singer during the 1930s.

In Lone Texas Ranger, Red Ryder pinned on a Ranger badge.

Moving to bit parts in Westerns, he was signed as a singing cowboy by PRC in 1945. The slender, affable singer made little impression as an action hero, and *The Tioga Kid* was his last starring role. (Tioga, a small Texas community north of Dallas, is Gene Autry's hometown.) Eddie Dean has dual roles: a Texas Ranger in pursuit of a band of rustlers, and a lookalike rustler called "The Tioga Kid." His sidekick is Roscoe Ates, and Jennifer Holt is the leading lady.

Republic Studios produced the best Ranger movie of 1948, *The Gallant Legion*, a feature film which ran for 88 minutes. Wild Bill Elliott starred as a Ranger opposing a plot to abolish the Ranger force and admit Texas into the Union in five sections, rather than as a single vast state. (The 1845 annexation agreement between the United States and the Republic of Texas actually provided the possibility of a five-way split, which would have created ten new U.S. senators from slave states, rather than merely two.) *The Gallant Legion* is a delight to watch, because of the cast of Western players assembled by Republic: Andy Devine, Bruce Cabot, Adrian Booth, Adele Mara, Kermit Maynard, Grant Withers, Hal Taliaferro, George Chesebro, Rex Lease, Iron Eyes Cody, Glenn Strange, and a host of others.

The most enjoyable Ranger film of 1949 was *Streets of Laredo*, a Technicolor remake of King Vidor's 1936 movie, *The Texas Rangers*. Paramount lensed the new version in 1949, starring handsome William Holden and beefy William Bendix as the outlaws who were transformed into Texas Rangers. Their old bandit pal is played with murderous wickedness by MacDonald Carey, who is clad in black. Pretty Mona Freeman is Holden's sweetheart, while bad guy Alfonso Bedoya is cheerfully wicked. Although the Comanche raiders are removed from this version, the storyline otherwise remains the same. A

Wild Bill Elliott played the last of his four Ranger roles in The Gallant Legion.

chilling moment involves Bendix and Carey, seated across a table from each other. Carey cold-bloodedly shoots his former comrade beneath the table. But Holden, aided by his rifle-wielding sweetheart, takes revenge on the evil Carey. *Streets of Laredo* is filled with action and Ranger camaraderie, and features a haunting score. While *The Texas Rangers* was an exciting Ranger film of the Texas Centennial year, *Streets of Laredo* brought an improved version of this Ranger tale to a later generation of movie-goers.

In Streets of Laredo, *MacDonald Carey (left) remains an outlaw, while his pals William Bendix (middle) and William Holden become Texas Rangers.*

In Charles Starrett's first film of 1949, *Bandits of El Dorado*, the Durango Kid fakes the murder of a Texas Ranger in order to learn how criminals are escaping into Mexico. Also in 1949 singing cowboy Monte Hale starred in two Ranger movies for Republic. Hale was a big, likeable Texan from San Angelo who was a Republic cowboy star from 1946 through 1950. In *Ranger of the Cherokee Strip*, Monte is a Texas Ranger who helps prove the innocence of a Cherokee fugitive. In *South of Rio* Monte is a former Ranger battling an outlaw gang which is running rampant in frontier Texas. Roy Barcroft is one of the villains in both films.

In 1949 the Lone Ranger finally reappeared onscreen—on small screens, located in a growing number of living rooms across America. Throughout the 1940s *The Lone Ranger* remained immensely popular on network radio. In 1941 Earle Graser, the longtime voice of the Lone Ranger, was killed in an auto accident. Announcer Brace Beemer then switched his resonant baritone to the title role, and then he played the Lone Ranger until the show ended in 1955. Fred Foy became the announcer, while John Todd was the voice of Tonto throughout the twenty-two-year run. Despite a vast and faithful radio

In 1949 Texan Monte Hale starred in two Ranger movies.

audience, however, the Lone Ranger disappeared from movie screens after *Hi-Yo Silver* in 1940, apparently because George Trendle disliked the changes Hollywood made in the characters he had created. But Trendle finally agreed to expand the Lone Ranger's audience into a new medium.

At 7:30 on Thursday evening, September 15, 1949, *The Lone Ranger* debuted on the ABC television network, which at this point, like other TV networks, went into homes only in the northeast and Midwest. *The Lone Ranger* was the first Western series filmed for television. A B-movie actor named Clayton Moore played the masked man, while Jay Silverheels, a Mohawk born in Canada, embodied Tonto. Silver was magnificent, even on the tiny screens of 1949, and so was the familiar story of the Ranger ambush by the Butch Cavendish Gang, retold in the premier episode.

When the small Ranger squad is warned against pursuing the large outlaw band, the proud reply is immediate: "Mister, the Rangers are used to long odds."

When the six Rangers, each wearing star-shields, ride in pursuit, Clayton Moore's face is never shown (throughout the entire series he was never seen without a mask except when wearing a beard or other disguise). Moore's older brother, Captain Dan Reid, was played by Tris Coffin. Another veteran of Ranger movies, bear-like Glenn Strange, played the evil Butch Cavendish, a recurring role for several episodes.

Following the ambush of the Rangers, the sole survivor—wounded in the face, which necessitated a bandana over his features—is nursed back to health by Tonto. "You all alone now," observes Tonto, after burying the other five Rangers. "Last man. You are Lone Ranger."

"Yes, Tonto. I am the Lone Ranger." A mask is fashioned

from the vest of his dead brother. A white stallion, gored by a buffalo, is found and tamed in Wild Horse Valley. The Lone Ranger now could begin his pursuit of Butch Cavendish and other outlaws.

During the last few months of 1949 viewers excitedly awaited each half-hour program on Thursdays. Indeed, *The Lone Ranger* would lead ABC-TV into the 1950s.

Clayton Moore starred as a masked man in a 1949 serial, The Ghost of Zorro, *a role instrumental in winning him the part of the Lone Ranger later that year on television.*

1940S

BEST RANGER MOVIES
The Ranger and the Lady (1940—Roy Rogers)
Last of the Duanes (1941—George Montgomery)
The Gallant Legion (1948—Wild Bill Elliott)
Streets of Laredo (1949—William Holden)

MOST FAMOUS MOVIE STAR IN A RANGER ROLE
Gary Cooper, *North West Mounted Police* (1940)

MOST MOVIE ROLES AS A RANGER: 22
Dave "Tex" O'Brien, The Texas Ranger Series

MOST YEARS STARRING IN A NEW RANGER MOVIE: 9
Charles Starrett, who made a Ranger film in
every year of the decade except 1948

FIRST COLOR MOVIE ABOUT A RANGER
North West Mounted Police (1940)

BEST RANGER TELEVISION SERIES
The Lone Ranger (ABC-TV, 1949 . . .)

BEST RANGER BOOK
Border Boss, Captain John R. Hughes—Texas Ranger
(1942—Jack Martin)

MOST POLITICALLY INCORRECT RANGER MOVIE MOMENT
Ranger Sgt. Gabby Hayes comparing his bag of
scalps, tribe by tribe, with that of a crony. *The Ranger
and The Lady* (1940—Roy Rogers)

RANGER EVENTS
Ranger force expanded to six companies, each with
a captain and a sergeant, and a total of 45 men (1941).
Six companies expanded to a total of 51 men (1947).
During World War II, Rangers sought out enemy aliens,
while instructing local police and civilians in the latest techniques of protecting factories, dams,
and generating plants from sabotage.

1950s: Rangers on TV

"Texas! More than 260,000 square miles! And fifty men who make up the most famous and oldest law enforcement body in North America!"
—Radio introduction to *Tales of the Texas Rangers*

*F*or years television broadcasts were received only by a few thousand primitive TV sets in New York. There were no daytime telecasts, and evening programming was random, without any regular "series." But rapid expansion occurred after World War II. In January 1949 NBC linked northeastern and midwest networks, and the link was completed to the west coast in September 1951. With nationwide television available, a forest of television antennas sprouted in towns and cities across America.

Western films always had been a staple of the motion picture industry, and television would turn to the same source of programming. Beginning in 1935, William Boyd had starred in sixty-six Hopalong Cassidy movies. Boyd cannily acquired television rights to his old films before television was considered to be of any significance. But in 1945 in New York Hopalong Cassidy films became the first movies shown on television, and Boyd launched a Hopalong Cassidy series on NBC-TV in 1949. Quick to spot a trend, Gene Autry commenced a half-

hour weekly program on CBS in 1950, while *The Roy Rogers Show* first appeared on NBC in 1951.

Hitting the airwaves in September 1949, *The Lone Ranger* quickly became ABC's biggest television hit. When the A. C. Nielsen Company began compiling national ratings for television network programs in 1950, *The Lone Ranger* was ABC's only program ranked in the Top 15. During the first season fifty-two episodes were filmed, going directly into the second season with twenty-six more episodes. From September 1949 until March 1951 there were new episodes each week, solidifying the viewing habits of young audiences.

With Clayton Moore in the title role, The Lone Ranger *became a hit in the early years of network TV.*

As television's Lone Ranger, thirty-five-year-old Clayton Moore experienced sudden stardom. Moore had begun his show business career as a trapeze performer before going to Hollywood in 1937. He appeared in B Westerns and serials, usually for Republic Studios. The role of a masked man in a 1949 serial, *The Ghost of Zorro*, convinced producers that Moore should star in *The Lone Ranger*. He found working conditions in early TV similar to B movies. In his autobiography, Moore stated that acting in *The Lone Ranger* offered the same challenges as the Bs: "too little time, too little money, but the show must go on." The first few half-hour episodes were filmed in two days (hour-long B Westerns usually were filmed within a week). Budgets were merely $12,500 per episode, gradually rising to $18,000 by 1954.

Moore handled fight scenes convincingly, and he was a fine rider, requesting widened stirrups so that he could execute running mounts. But his line delivery was wooden and pedantic. In 1951, after two seasons and seventy-eight episodes, Clayton Moore was dropped from the series. John Hart was cast as the new Lone Ranger, wearing an enlarged mask as an effort to conceal the change. Hart starred in fifty-two episodes, from September 1952 through September 1953. Daytime reruns began on Saturdays in June 1953, later moving to Sunday afternoons and, in 1960-1961, on Wednesday afternoons. New half-hour episodes resumed in the Thursday evening time slot at 7:30 on September 9, 1954—with Clayton Moore again behind the mask.

"No one connected with *The Lone Ranger* ever told me why I had been fired," related Clayton Moore in his autobiography, "and I never asked." During the two years he was away from *The Lone Ranger*, Moore returned to movie work, usually in

supporting roles featuring such Western stars as Gene Autry, Tim Holt and Charles Starrett. But fan mail to television producers steadily protested his absence from *The Lone Ranger*,

John Hart played the Lone Ranger on TV during the 1952-53 season. The mask was enlarged so that it would be harder to tell that the Lone Ranger was not Clayton Moore.

and in 1954 he was invited to return to the series. "I was back on *The Lone Ranger* set by early June 1954."

For fifty-two weeks, from September 1954 until September 1955, there were new episodes starring Clayton Moore. Although budgets remained limited, *The Lone Ranger* sometimes went on location at Old Tucson, and there was greater emphasis on the Lone Ranger donning disguises. On September 13, 1956, a new season began with thirty-nine color episodes. The final new episode, "Outlaws in Greasepaint," aired on June 6, 1957. There had been 221 episodes of *The Lone Ranger* filmed for TV. The color episodes would be rerun for decades, and television popularity would lead to new big screen versions of the Lone Ranger story.

The success of *The Lone Ranger* inspired another program for radio and TV audiences during the 1950s. Producer-director Stacy Keach (father of actor Stacy Keach, Jr.) traveled to Texas for research with a writer. Keach met with the most famous of all Texas Rangers, Captain Manuel "Lone Wolf" Gonzaullas. Keach engaged Captain Gonzaullas as the show's technical advisor, then traveled 1,500 miles across the Lone Star State, observing the Rangers in field operations.

Keach lined up an established Western star for the role of Ranger Jace Pearson. By 1950 Joel McCrea had been a Hollywood leading man for two decades. He was born in Los Angeles in 1905, and he went on to attend Hollywood High. In the summers he worked at California ranches and became a superb horseman.

When he was fourteen, McCrea began appearing as an extra in silent films, including a few Westerns. McCrea was tall and ruggedly handsome, with a sense of integrity that came through on the big screen. By the 1930s he was a leading man

Popular western star Joel McCrea played Ranger Jace Pearson on the radio series, Tales of the Texas Rangers.

in comedies and dramas. In 1937 he had his first starring role in a Western, *Wells Fargo*, and two years later, Cecil B. DeMille cast him in *Union Pacific*. McCrea played the title role in *Buffalo Bill* in 1944 and in the fourth remake of *The Virginian* in 1946. At this point he began working almost exclusively in Westerns, starring in five in 1949.

With Joel McCrea lending star power, *Tales of the Texas Rangers* debuted over the NBC Radio Network on July 8, 1950. The thirty-minute show, sponsored by Wheaties, ran on Saturday nights at 9:30 for three months. In October the show switched to Sunday evenings, eventually settling into the six o'clock time slot.

"Tales of the Texas Rangers, starring Joel McCrea as Ranger Jace Pearson!" proclaimed announcer Hal Gibney at the opening of each weekly show. "Texas! More than 260,000 square miles!" continued Gibney. "And fifty men who make up the most famous and oldest law enforcement body in North America! Now, from the files of the Texas Rangers, come these stories based on fact. Only names, dates and places are fictitious for obvious reasons; the events themselves are a matter of record."

The weekly adventures were set during the previous two decades, so that the show would have a modern slant. Ranger Jace Pearson drove an automobile, but he had a horse trailer, and sometimes galloped into the back country aboard Charcoal—the name of Gonzaullas' horse—in pursuit of lawbreakers. The familiar voice of Joel McCrea was warm but authoritative, and listeners readily identified the movie star's face with that of Ranger Pearson.

After two seasons, *Tales of the Texas Rangers* concluded its radio run on September 14, 1952. But within a few years, as

Western series began to proliferate on television, *Tales of the Texas Rangers* was dusted off for TV. At first intended for juvenile audiences, a *Tales of the Texas Rangers* theme song was recorded by Shorty Long for RCA's Children's Bluebird Records. This theme song proclaimed the Rangers to be "a band of sturdy men." A *Tales of the Texas Rangers* comic book also was published.

Joel McCrea, still starring in Hollywood Westerns, was unavailable for a juvenile TV series. Tall Willard Parker assumed the role of Jace Pearson, while co-star Harry Lauter played Ranger Clay Morgan. Unlike the radio version, television episodes alternated between the 1950s and frontier Texas.

From 1955 through 1958 *Tales of the Texas Rangers* was aired in the afternoons over CBS-TV. In the fall of 1958 ABC-TV picked up the half-hour show, running it at five o'clock on Thursday afternoons. But by this time Westerns had reached a peak of popularity on primetime television. So on December 22, 1958, ABC moved *Tales of the Texas Rangers* to 7:30 on Monday evenings. Parker and Lauter could not carry the show in primetime, however, and *Tales of the Texas Rangers* was cancelled after the May 25, 1959, episode.

While *Tales of the Texas Rangers* and *The Lone Ranger* were coming into homes via radio and TV, movie theaters ran a number of Ranger films during the early 1950s. In 1950 Don "Red" Barry starred in *Border Rangers*. The following year Tim Holt made another Ranger movie as part of the RKO series, *Law of the Badlands*.

In 1951 Charles Starrett added to his long list of Ranger films with two excellent Durango Kid films: big, handsome "Steve," who periodically would vanish, whereupon the Durango Kid would appear, clad in black outfit and disguised

Charles Starrett as the Durango Kid, the "Robin Hood of the West." In the Durango Kid movies, Starrett played a cowboy named Steve, who would change into a black outfit and don a mask to battle bad guys. In several of these movies Steve was a Texas Ranger.

by a black bandana and mask. In *Prairie Roundup* Steve is an ex-Ranger who devises an elaborate plan to foil a gang of cattle rustlers. Steve "murders" the Durango Kid and is thrown in jail. But Steve's sidekick, Smiley Burnette, helps him escape, and they hire on with pretty Mary Castle, whose ranch is a target of the rustlers. Starrett's next film was *Ridin' the Outlaw Trail*. This time Steve is an active Texas Ranger (as well as, of course, the Durango Kid), while Smiley Burnette is an inept comic blacksmith. After a thief steals $20,000 in gold coins, he is murdered, and his killer melts the coins into gold that he claims has just been discovered. Ranger Steve and the Durango Kid take less than an hour to unravel this scheme.

In 1951 George Montgomery starred in The Texas Rangers, *his fourth Ranger movie.*

Another 1951 Ranger flick starred Easterner Mickey Rooney, who travels to "Texas" (the movie was filmed in Mexico City) to find his brother, played by Robert Stack. Encountering Texas Ranger Robert Preston, Rooney discovers that his brother is an outlaw. *My Brother the Outlaw* is silly screen fare, despite a vigorous performance as a Texas Ranger by Preston.

A somewhat more serious Ranger movie, *The Texas Rangers*, purported to present an historic account of the manhunt for the Sam Bass Gang. George Montgomery—one of the five masked men in the original Lone Ranger serial—is an ex-convict who was framed by the Sundance Kid. The

The Other Rangers on Film

Although greatly overshadowed by their Texas counterparts, the Arizona Rangers carved out a brief but exciting law enforcement record during the final years of the Wild West. From 1901 to 1909 the Rangers overwhelmed the outlaws of Arizona Territory, which persuaded Congress to grant long-delayed statehood. The Arizona lawmen openly copied the methods of the Texas Rangers, and nearly half of their enrollment was comprised of Texans, including several former Rangers.

The Arizona Rangers were disbanded after less than eight years of service, but their exploits were reflected in an occasional film. In 1933, Bob Steele made a B-Western called *Trailin' North*. The opening scene is at a "Ranger Station," where Bob learns that his father figure, an Arizona Ranger, has been fatally wounded. "When a Ranger hits a trail to bring back desperate men," states the Ranger captain, "in many cases he pays for it with his life." Bob is handed the man's badge (a shield totally unlike the numbered star worn by real Rangers), and rides in pursuit of the killer. Within three weeks Ranger Bob has trekked to Alaska, abandoning his horse for snowshoes and a dogsled, and trading his broad-brimmed hat for a fur cap. The murderer, Slash Ryan (played by George—pre-Gabby—Hayes) is killed by Ranger Bob in a final shootout.

The Arizona Ranger was filmed in 1948 and co-starred Tim Holt and his father, Jack Holt. Appropriately Jack and Tim played father and son in the movie. Jack is an Arizona rancher and Tim is a Spanish-American War veteran who returns home with two fellow Rough Rider friends. Tim and his buddies accept appointment as Arizona Rangers (there was an actual Ranger-Rough Rider connection), and Jack eventually helps them round up the bad guys.

A decade later, in 1958, ABC-TV produced a weekly series based on the adventures of the Arizona Rangers. *26 Men* (a reference to the authorized strength of the Rangers) starred tall, silver-haired Tris Coffin as Capt. Tom Rynning, who commanded the company from 1902-1907. But *26 Men* ran for only one season—the Arizona Rangers have never captured either television or movie audiences.

Kid is played by Ian McDonald (the murderous Frank Miller in *High Noon*), while Sam Bass is portrayed by William Bishop. There is a great deal of action in Trucolor, but the "history" is not very historic—about like most Texas Ranger films. A comic book version of the movie also was released in 1951.

The following year Gene Autry made *Night Stage to Galveston* for Columbia (Autry had changed studios, from Republic to Columbia, in 1947). Gene and sidekick Pat Buttram are former Rangers who have become newspapermen crusading against police corruption in Texas. Their publisher's daughter, played by Virginia Huston, is kidnapped by the bad guys, forcing Gene and Pat to revert to their Ranger ways. In featured roles were Robert Livingston and Clayton Moore, who each had played the Lone Ranger. There is a lack of action, so the hour-long film is filled out with such songs as *Eyes of Texas*, *Yellow Rose of Texas*, and *A Heart as Big as Texas*.

Gene Autry and Columbia produced another Ranger film in 1953, *Winning of the West*. Gene is a Texas Ranger who discovers his brother among an outlaw gang which sells "protection" to miners and townspeople. When Gene refuses to shoot his brother he temporarily loses his badge. But Gene finally wins back his brother, who helps him round up the bad guys. Smiley Burnette returns as Gene's sidekick, perky Gail Davis is the leading lady, and former Lone Ranger Robert Livingston has another featured role.

Also in 1953 Wayne Morris starred as a Texas Ranger in *Star of Texas*, the first film of an Allied Artist series. Wild Bill Elliott was supposed to star in the six films, but when he became unavailable, Wayne Morris was given the lead. Morris was a strapping blond who had flown nearly sixty missions as a Navy pilot during World War II. Morris is a Ranger who goes

undercover to thwart an outlaw hang led by Paul Fix. The pace of the film is fast-moving, but the production values are spare and cheap-looking.

Star of Texas proved to be the first entry of the final series of B Western films. The last B Western, *Two Guns and a Badge*, was released in 1954. The steady stream of television Westerns rendered B Westerns obsolete. After 1954, any Ranger movies would have to be feature-length Westerns.

In 1956 Warner Brothers released a Western feature: *The Lone Ranger*, starring Clayton Moore and Jay Silverheels. Jake Wrather, a wealthy businessman, had purchased all rights to the Lone Ranger from creator George Trendle for $3 million. In addition to the TV and radio shows, *The Lone Ranger* comic books sold two million copies each month, and *The Lone Ranger* comic strip ran in 300 newspapers. Wrather, who was married to movie actress Bonita Granville, soon decided to extend the Lone Ranger onto movie screens. Warner Brothers began filming in 1955, with location shooting at Kanab, Utah. Clayton Moore was unaccustomed to the careful pace of filmmaking at a major studio: "it seemed like a vacation to us."

Moore and Jay Silverheels provided familiar casting. Bonita Granville was the innocent wife of the boss villain, a greedy and ambitious rancher played by Lyle Bettger. Another veteran bad guy, burly Robert Wilke, portrayed Bettger's murderous foreman, who finally kills his own boss. A nostalgic cast member was Lane Chandler, who had been a Ranger in both the 1938 and 1939 Lone Ranger serials.

Filmed in color, *The Lone Ranger* is a handsome Western, with widescreen scenes of cattle drives and Indian camps and precipitous canyons. Early in the film the Lone Ranger tells the territorial governor the story of the ambush of the Butch

Cavendish Gang. During the course of the movie Tonto is mobbed and lynched, but the Lone Ranger arrives in time to part the hanging rope with a silver bullet. At one point the Lone Ranger is wounded, and he also wins a desperate hand-to-hand fight with a warrior named Angry Horse. In several scenes the Lone Ranger masquerades as a bearded oldtimer. There is a great deal of action, and fans enjoyed the best production values ever lavished upon a Lone Ranger film.

Western movie expert Brian Garfield conceded that *The Lone Ranger* was "strictly for kiddies, but well made in color for theatrical release and not just a compilation of TV footage." Another fine Western critic, Phil Hardy, rated *The*

Lobby card for the 1956 color motion picture, The Lone Ranger.

Lone Ranger as: "A masterpiece of children's cinema." Reviews were good and attendance was strong. Clayton Moore and Silver went on a publicity tour through thirty-three cities, further spreading the Lone Ranger image.

Although *The Lone Ranger* ended thirty-one years on radio in 1954 and the television series shut down in 1957, the success of the 1956 movie called for a sequel. Not long after finishing his television work as the Lone Ranger. Clayton Moore was summoned back to Hollywood for *The Lone Ranger and the Lost City of Gold*. United Artists backed the project, which was filmed on location in Old Tucson.

Before the opening credits, an introductory sequence depicted the Cavendish ambush, the arrival of Tonto and Silver, and the creation of the Lone Ranger. When the thirty-nine color episodes of television's Lone Ranger were re-edited into thirteen videos, this explanatory sequence introduced each video.

Unfortunately, the brief introduction was the best scene in *The Lone Ranger and the Lost City of Gold*. Although the color shots of the southern Arizona vistas give the film an excellent look, there is little action. *The Lone Ranger* featured one exciting scene after another, but a new director and screenwriters slowed the pace of *The Lone Ranger and the Lost City of Gold* to a crawl. As the story limps along, the Lone Ranger—as usual—dons a disguise. Although Tonto receives a scalp wound, he soon recovers to help the Lone Ranger foil a band of masked raiders. The head villain (Douglas Kennedy) is murdered by the villainess (Noreen Nash), who then is captured by the Lone Ranger.

There would be no sequel to this lackluster 1958 film. By now the Lone Ranger was off television, except for reruns.

Although Clayton Moore would continue to make personal appearances—and TV commercials—as the masked man, he no longer would film further adventures of the Lone Ranger.

The next year an excellent Ranger movie was made from a superb novel. *The Wonderful Country* was published in 1952 by Texas artist and author Tom Lea, who illustrated the book with striking drawings. *The Wonderful Country* is set along the Rio Grande on the southwestern Texas frontier. The central character is Martin Brady, a hard-bitten *americano* who has worked across the border as a *pistolero* for gunrunners for several years, but feels drawn back to his native land. On the American side are cavalrymen, warriors, and Company E of the Frontier Battalion of Texas Rangers. Early in the story Captain John Rucker arrives with his family to take command of Company E. Brady is in the midst of conflicts between Mexicans, Rangers, Apaches, and cavalrymen. And his problems include involvement with the cavalry commander's wife. Captain Rucker enlists Brady as a Ranger, and following a climactic shootout, he crosses back into Texas for good.

The Wonderful Country offered complex characters, intriguing subplots and realistic situations. Popular movie star Robert Mitchum acquired the novel as a property for his new production company, and *The Wonderful Country* became his second film. Mitchum was compelling and powerful as Martin Brady. Albert Dekker, who played a Texas Ranger in *Rangers of Fortune* (1940), was Ranger Captain John Rucker. Gary Merrill was the cavalry major and singer Julie London was his wife. Pedro Armendariz was excellent as a petty Mexican tyrant, and Charles McGraw was gruff but likeable as the town doctor who befriended Brady. Legendary baseball pitcher Satchel Paige played a sergeant of "buffalo soldiers," while author Tom Lea

Robert Mitchum, with co-star Julie London, in The Wonderful Country, *one of the finest Ranger movies ever filmed.*

had a small part as a barber. It was a strong cast, and the color photography added stark beauty to the 1959 film.

The Wonderful Country is one of the finest Ranger movies ever filmed. But an even better motion picture involving Texas Rangers already had been released during the 1950s. In 1956 *The Searchers* was lensed by John Ford, greatest of all Western directors. Ford won Academy Awards for films other than Westerns, but *The Searchers* was his Western masterpiece. And starring in *The Searchers* was the greatest of all Western actors, John Wayne.

1950s

BEST RANGER MOVIES
The Searchers (1956—John Wayne)
The Lone Ranger (1956—Clayton Moore)
The Wonderful Country (1959—Tom Lea)

BEST NEW RANGER RADIO SERIES
Tales of the Texas Rangers (1950-52—Joel McCrea)

BEST NEW RANGER TELEVISION PROGRAM
Tales of the Texas Rangers (1958-59—Willard Parker)

BEST RANGER BOOKS
The Wonderful Country (1952—Tom Lea)
The Comancheros (1952—Paul I. Wellman)
The Searchers (1954—Alan LeMay)

RANGER EVENTS
Texas Rangers enjoyed a continuity of leadership under the lengthy supervision (1935-69) of Colonel Homer Garrison, Jr. With an authorized strength of fifty-one men throughout the 1950s, the Rangers investigated over 8,000 cases each year.

John Wayne and the Texas Rangers

"Mount! Mount! M-o-n-t-e, mount!"
—Orders from Ranger Captain Sam Clayton
(Ward Bond, *The Searchers*)

D uring a fabled career in which he appeared in more than 150 motion pictures, John Wayne starred in scores of Westerns and became the silver screen's greatest Western star. From *The Alamo* to *Texas Terror* to *Three Texas Steers*, many of Duke's Western films were set in the Lone Star State. During the 1930s, when he filmed dozens of B Westerns, John Wayne frequently rode the Texas range, but not as a member of the world's most famous law enforcement body. He was either a Texas cowboy or an "undercover man" or a "special agent," appointed by the governor.

After the Duke became a major star, he enjoyed a Texas Ranger connection in three of his finest films. In 1956 John Wayne starred as rugged, hard-bitten Ethan Edwards in *The Searchers*. Directed by the legendary John Ford, *The Searchers* is regarded by film critics as one of the greatest Westerns ever lensed. The movie was based on a stark, gripping novel of the same title by Alan LeMay. Set on the Texas frontier after the Civil War, *The Searchers* centered on the Edwards family. Still

wearing remnants of his Confederate cavalry uniform, Ethan Edwards returns to his brother's ranch. Undercurrents of the family reunion include an unspoken love between Ethan and his brother's wife, and Ethan's vague racist discomfort with Martin Pawley, played by Jeffrey Hunter. Years earlier the Pawley family had been massacred by Comanches, and little Martin was rescued by Ethan. Although Martin was one-eighth Cherokee, the orphan was raised on the Edwards ranch.

The morning after Ethan's return, a small band of Texas Rangers and settlers arrive at the ranch while pursuing Comanche raiders. The Rangers are captained by Reverend Sam Clayton, forcefully portrayed by Ward Bond. The Reverend Captain Clayton combines religious and military duties, protecting his frontier society after the pattern of righteous Old Testament leaders. Captain Clayton swears in Ethan and Martin as Temporary Rangers, although Ethan grumbles that he already swore an oath to the Confederacy.

John Wayne and Ward Bond, who played a colorful Texas Ranger captain in the Western classic, The Searchers.

But while Clayton's men ride in pursuit, the Comanches double back to strike the Edwards ranch. The family is brutally slain, although the youngest daughter is carried off by the Comanches. Ethan and Martin commence a five-year search for Debbie Edwards, a dangerous odyssey fueled by Ethan's loathing of Comanches. When Debbie finally is located, Ethan and Martin help Captain Clayton and a small Ranger company attack the Comanche camp, and Debbie is rescued.

Also participating in the climactic assault is a contingent of the U.S. Cavalry. But the cavalrymen are considerably less experienced at fighting Indians than the Rangers, and ride under the direction of Captain Clayton. Historically, this situation is reminiscent of the 1850s, when the newly-organized U.S. Cavalry learned techniques of fighting horseback warriors while riding alongside veteran Texas Rangers. Captain Clayton is in command of Ranger Company A, "all fourteen of 'em," and they are paid "twelve Yankee dollars a month." With typical Ranger courage, members of this understrength company are undismayed by superior Comanche numbers. When the Rangers become hemmed in by Comanche riders, Captain Clayton bellows that "I aim to get unsurrounded!" In the novel there are forty-two Rangers, and the captain tells them they are lucky: "For once we got enough Comanches to go around."

Alan LeMay's 1954 novel, based on the search of Brit Johnson, an African-American cowboy, for members of his family and that of his lady boss, was harsh and grim. Director John Ford decided to provide comic relief with three characters: Old Mose, played by gangly Hank Worden; Ranger Charlie MacCorry, played by Ford's son-in-law, Ken Curtis, who utilized the hayseed caricature he had developed while singing with the Sons of the Pioneers (Curtis later used this

characterization to create Festus Haggen for *Gunsmoke*); and Ranger Captain Sam Clayton.

In LeMay's novel, the Ranger leader is named Sol Clinton. During the span of the novel Clinton rises from lieutenant to captain, and Charlie MacCorry is promoted from private to sergeant. (MacCorry also marries Laurie Mathison in the novel; but in the movie Laurie winds up with Martin Pawley). In LeMay's novel, Clinton, MacCorry and another Ranger come to a barn dance. "There were three of them, and they made their arrival inconspicuous. They wore no uniform—the Rangers had none—and their badges were in their pockets." In addition to this description, LeMay added the general opinion: "Rangers were a good thing, and there ought to be more of them. Sometimes you need a company of them badly."

John Ford changed Sol Clinton's name to Sam Clayton, and he added the vocation of rural preacher to the captain's Ranger duties. Ford also changed the name of the lead character, from Amos Edwards to Ethan. As Ethan Edwards, John Wayne turned in perhaps the most powerful performance of his career, sustaining a grim ferocity throughout the film. But Ward Bond, registering a loud and confident sense of authority, frequently matches Wayne's strength, while adding occasional touches of warmth and humor as the area's preacher. Bond appears early and then late in *The Searchers*, and each appearance enlivens the movie. As Captain Clayton, Bond is everything a frontier Ranger leader should be: decisive, bold, courageous, resourceful, and a tower of strength. If *The Searchers* offers John Wayne's finest performance, the movie also shows Ward Bond at his best. Among the many triumphs of *The Searchers*, this classic Western presents a superb characterization of a Ranger captain and his resolute band of men.

Ward Bond, Ranger Captain

Ward Bond played a captain of Texas Rangers in one of the best Westerns ever filmed. A veteran of nearly fifty Westerns, along with various other movies, Bond was fifty-one when *The Searchers* was lensed. Big and rugged, Bond became a 220-pound tackle on the USC football squad. A teammate, Michael Morrison (who would adopt the stage name John Wayne), dropped out of college to seek movie work, and Bond soon followed. Both young men were boisterous and fun-loving, and they became close friends. They also became friendly with director John Ford, and they were key members of the "John Ford Stock Company."

While John Wayne rose to superstardom, Ward Bond became one of Hollywood's best known character actors. He was a loud, forceful part of such memorable films as *It Happened One Night* (Best Picture of 1934), *Drums Along the Mohawk*, *Unconquered*, *Young Mr. Lincoln*, and *The Quiet Man*. One of his first Westerns was with Buck Jones in 1934, *The Fighting Ranger*. Through the years he appeared in such fine Westerns as *Dodge City*, *The Oklahoma Kid*, *Virginia City*, *Santa Fe Trail*, *My Darling Clementine*, *Fort Apache*, *Three Godfathers*, *Wagonmaster*, *Hondo*, and *Rio Bravo*. Bond finally became a leading man on television in 1957, as Major Seth Adams on the popular series *Wagon Train*.

When John Ford asked him to create a key character for *The Searchers*, Bond channeled his experience and talents into the role of Captain-Reverend Samuel Clayton.

Five years later John Wayne played a Ranger captain in *The Comancheros*, the only film in his long career in which he wore the badge of a Texas Ranger. Based on the 1952 historical novel by Paul I. Wellman, *The Comancheros* centers on the traders in West Texas called Comancheros who supplied Comanches with rifles and other goods. Wellman's story begins in 1843 in New Orleans, from where gambler Paul Regret is forced to flee following a duel. Entering the Republic of Texas, the urbane Regret is taken aback by the raw, primitive conditions, which the author expertly describes. Scenes in Washington-on-the-Brazos and the capital village of Austin offer accurate depictions, and Wellman deftly captures the larger-than-life president of Texas, Sam Houston.

President Houston permits the sharp-shooting Regret to enlist in the Rangers rather than suffer extradition to Louisiana. Private Regret is sent to a frontier outpost, where he observes his new comrades. "At this post were stationed about fifty men, hard-looking and uncouth, most of them bearded, and lean to the point of cadaverous. But in them he noticed one thing in common: a certain steadiness of eye, and a peculiar competence, especially with weapons or when mounted." The company is ably commanded by Captain Blake Henrion. Private Tom Gatling, the tall, dour Ranger who had apprehended Regret, openly dislikes the Louisiana fugitive.

Following a series of ferocious Comanche raids, President Houston sends Henrion, Gatling, and Regret to West Texas. The Rangers pose as outlaws on the run, and are taken to Comanchero headquarters at Palo Duro Canyon. Regret encounters a sweetheart from New Orleans, who is the daughter of the head Comanchero. The identity of the Rangers is discovered, but a Ranger company arrives at Palo Duro Canyon after

a long pursuit of Comanche raiders. Although desperately out-numbered, the Rangers engage in battle. Henrion and Gatling are killed, but Regret drills Chief Iron Shirt, and the Comanches ride away in dismay and confusion.

John Wayne agreed to star in the movie version, but his Texas Ranger character would not die in the end. (In *The Searchers*, Amos Edwards was killed in the novel's final battle, but John Wayne's Ethan Edwards was still standing when the movie screen announced "The End.") In *The Comancheros*, Wayne played Captain Jake Cutter, a cross between Captain Blake Henrion and big Tim Gatling. Wayne's Captain Jake is formidable, but unlike the reserved Captain Henrion or the ill-tempered Gatling, he is genial and good-natured. Captain Jake even has a romance with beautiful Joan O'Brien, whose de-ceased husband and Jake fought under General Sam Houston at San Jacinto. Captain Jake remains alive at the end of *The Comancheros*, presumably so that he can resume his courtship of the lovely blond widow.

The movie is set in 1843 and generally followed the story-line of the novel, although the Rangers are armed with Winchesters and cartridge revolvers from a much later period. The Rangers heroically battle Comanche warriors, and eventu-ally destroy the Comanche hideout. *The Comancheros* is packed with rousing action and colorful characters. Lee Marvin almost steals the movie as a wild, vicious villain—until he is shot to death by Captain Jake. Character actor Edgar Buchanan portrays a reprobate judge based on the legendary Roy Bean. The old cowboy star Bob Steele, a boyhood friend of the Duke, plays a Texas rancher. The Duke's son, Pat Wayne, plays a young Ranger (Pat also was a young cavalry lieutenant in *The Searchers*). Handsome Stuart Whitman is the embodiment of Paul Regret.

John Wayne was genial but strong as Texas Ranger Captain Jake Cutter in The Comancheros.

But *The Comancheros* belonged to John Wayne. At the opening credits Wayne is on horseback, overlooking a vast canyon, while Elmer Bernstein's magnificent theme music throbbed through the theater. The scene was worth the price of admission by itself. *The Comancheros* is one of John Wayne's most entertaining movies, offering a slam-bang portrayal of Texas Rangers that, like most other Ranger films, is longer on action than historical accuracy.

In 1969 the Duke starred in another Western with a Ranger connection, *True Grit*. Like his other Ranger movies, *True Grit* was based on an excellent novel, published in 1968. Author Charles Portis, revealing an artful ear for period dialogue, created a delightful cast of characters and one of the funniest Westerns ever penned. The novel is written in first person, with elderly spinster Mattie Ross recounting her adventures at the age of fourteen after her father is murdered in Fort Smith, Arkansas. The killer, Tom Chaney, also is wanted for murder in Texas, and he flees into the lawless wilderness of Indian Territory.

Spunky and opinionated, Mattie leaves the family farm to recover her father's body, then decides to pursue Tom Chaney. She employs Rooster Cogburn, a one-eyed, quick-triggered deputy U.S. marshal. They are joined by "a Sergeant of Texas Rangers, working out of a place called Ysleta near El Paso." The Ranger, Sergeant LaBouef, wears flashy Mexican spurs and a two-gun rig, and he carries a Sharps "Big Fifty" buffalo rifle. Tom Chaney had murdered a Texas state senator, and Sergeant LaBouef was detached from his regular duties to pursue the killer. Mattie regards LaBouef as "a vain and cocky devil," and Rooster also dislikes him. But Tom Chaney has joined the outlaw gang of Lucky Ned Pepper, and Rooster de-

cides that another gun is needed, especially after La Bouef offers to share the substantial Texas reward. The two lawmen frequently wrangle during the pursuit. But during the final shootout an injured LaBouef kills Lucky Ned Pepper with a long-range shot from his Sharps to save Rooster. "The distance covered by LaBouef's wonderful shot at the moving rider was over six hundred yards," marvels Mattie. In the novel LaBouef packs Tom Chaney's body back to Texas, but in the movie the Ranger dies of his injuries. Either way, the honor of the

In True Grit *John Wayne won an Oscar as crusty Rooster Cogburn, Kim Darby played young Mattie Ross, and Glen Campbell somewhat awkwardly portrayed a Texas Ranger named La Boeuf.*

Take That Horse to the Woodshed!

To emphasize his imposing stature onscreen, John Wayne often handled a scaled-down rifle and ducked beneath low doorways. In *True Grit*, the big star rode a tall horse, while Glen Campbell was placed aboard a small mount for contrast.

In his autobiography, *Rhinestone Cowboy*, Campbell relates that he was assigned an even smaller horse, and when he rode alongside Wayne, the Duke towered above him. Furthermore, Wayne's aggressive animal intimidated Campbell's little horse, sometimes biting the pony on the neck. Campbell's mount, which had a hard time keeping up with the Duke's long-legged horse, soon began to shy away as well.

One wrangler, exasperated at the ornery behavior of the large horse, finally hit him in the head with a two-by-four after another biting incident. This direct lesson in equine manners worked. During the remainder of filming, when the two lawmen rode together, it was Wayne who had to work the reins to keep his big horse from shying away from Campbell's little mount.

Rangers is upheld by LaBouef, who saves Rooster by his skill with firearms.

The movie role of LaBouef was assigned to Country Western music superstar Glen Campbell, who was at the height of his popularity, and who sang a title ballad over the credits. Campbell looked good in the role, but he proved to be an inept actor. His awkward portrayal of LaBouef made the Ranger character seem genuinely unlikable.

Later, Campbell good-naturedly joked that "I made John Wayne look so good in *True Grit* that he won his only Oscar." Movie critic Gene Shalit observed, "Glen Campbell has never acted in films before and his record is still clean."

Wayne, by contrast, played Rooster Cogburn to the hilt. The star portrayed Rooster as a hard man in a dangerous world, with a rough sense of humor and a mean streak, re-lieved by occasional kindnesses to Mattie, or "Little Sister," as he called her. (Mattie was played by Kim Darby, who demon-strated some of the character's barbed qualities.)

The Duke's most memorable scene came late in *True Grit*. Rooster put the reins of his horse in his teeth, then charged the outlaw gang, gunning down the bad guys with a revolver in each hand. At the end of the fight Rooster, trapped by his fallen horse, is saved by the long rifle shot from the Ranger which finishes Ned Pepper (played by the superb Robert Duvall, who would give a notable performance as *Lonesome Dove*'s Captain Gus McCrae two decades later).

The movie closes with Rooster and his new horse jumping a fence at Mattie's farm. A freeze frame shows that the Duke—not a stunt man—is astride the mount. John Wayne received his only Academy Award for his role in *True Grit*—perhaps he should have filmed more movies that included Texas Rangers!

1960s–1970s:
Ranger Light—
Comedies and Cartoons

"Come all ye Texas Rangers/Wherever you may be
"I'll tell you of some troubles/That happened to me."
                              —Sung gamely by the retired Rangers
                              of *The Over-The-Hill Gang*

Although radio series programming had ended by the
1960s, and B Western movie series also had ceased
production, feature films and television continued to offer
popular venues for Ranger entertainment. Throughout the
1960s Western features continued to be a significant part of
motion picture product, and there were several Ranger movies
during the decade. Television provided American homes with
a steady diet of *Lone Ranger* reruns, along with various new
Western series and, with increasing frequency, Made For TV
movies. Film images of Texas Rangers would continue to be
available to the public during the 1960s.

But political assassinations, racial unrest, and the Vietnam
War began to take a toll on Western entertainment, among
many other elements of American society. There was wide-
spread distrust of America's heritage and traditional values, of

government and authority figures. During the late 1970s the number of Western films sharply declined, and Western series virtually disappeared from television. Texas Rangers, universally known as authority figures and upholders of law and order, ceased to be popular entertainment subjects. When Rangers did appear on film, they usually were objects of comedy (*The Great Bank Robbery*, *Laredo*, *The Over the Hill Gang*, etc.) or even ridicule (Capt. Frank Hamer in Bonnie and Clyde).

In 1960, when most Americans were as yet unaware of Vietnam and three years before the assassination of President John F. Kennedy, a traditional movie about brave and determined Texas Rangers was released. Native Texan Audie Murphy played a Ranger recruit in *Seven Ways From Sundown*. During World War II Murphy was heavily engaged in combat in Europe and was awarded thirty-three decorations for valor, including the Medal of Honor. Following the war Hollywood beckoned America's most decorated soldier. Although Murphy was untrained as an actor, he had boyish good looks and a national reputation. Despite his short stature, Murphy was completely believable as an action hero because audiences knew he had performed valorous deeds in real life. Murphy appeared in more than forty movies before his death in a plane crash in 1971. A majority of his films were Westerns, and he made a number of low budget oaters that might be regarded as latter-day B Westerns. Murphy was a film veteran by 1960; *Seven Ways From Sundown* was his thirtieth motion picture.

The name of Murphy's character was Seven Jones, short for Seven-Ways-From-Sundown Jones. Seven's parents worked the number of each child into their names. His older brother, Two Jones, had been a Texas Ranger until killed through the

Audie Murphy, Texan war hero, played Ranger Seven Jones in Seven Ways From Sundown.

cowardice of Ranger Lieutenant Herly, played by Ken Tobey. Unaware of Herly's role in the death of his brother, Ranger recruit Seven Jones reports for duty to the lieutenant. Herly assigns the rookie to track down a dangerous killer, Jim Flood. A Ranger sergeant named Hennessey, who once saved Flood's life, rides with young Jones.

Two excellent actors, Barry Sullivan and John McIntire, played Jim Flood and Sergeant Hennessey. Sullivan, as a genial but lethal gambler, overshadowed the rest of the cast with a charming performance.

When Seven and Hennessey take up Flood's trail, Jones observes that he's good with a rifle but not with a "revolving gun." During their far-ranging pursuit, the old sergeant tutors Jones in handling a pistol. But Hennessey is fatally wounded when Flood ambushes the men who are following him. Jones angrily rides within sight of Flood and drops the fleeing outlaw with one shot.

Seven takes his wounded prey to a cabin and nurses him, so that the fugitive can make the return journey and face legal justice. Flood is deeply remorseful when he learns that he has killed Hennessey, but repeatedly he tells Seven that he will not submit to being hanged. When Flood is ready to travel, the two men encounter numerous dangers on the long voyage back to Texas. Allowing Flood the temporary use of a gun, Seven and his prisoner fight off Apache warriors, bounty hunters, and a set of brothers seeking the killer. They survive other perils as well, and each man saves the other's life.

Seven finally jails Flood in Texas. But Flood has concealed a gun and shoots his way free. As he gallops out of town he wounds a young woman (two lovely actresses, Venetia Stevenson and Suzanne Lloyd, decorate the movie). Seven

soon confronts Flood, who tries to persuade the Ranger to join him in outlaw endeavors. Although Flood says he is sorry for shooting an innocent woman, Seven states that he cannot go through life being sorry. Flood and Seven like each other but are on opposite sides of the law. In the ensuing gunfight Ranger Seven does his duty and kills the bad guy.

Texan Audie Murphy was convincing as an earnest young Ranger in a solid film. Incidentally, Murphy played a frontier Texan in another 1960 Western, *The Unforgiven*. *The Unforgiven* was based on a novel by Alan LeMay (*The Searchers*) and starred Burt Lancaster and Audrey Hepburn. John Huston, one of Hollywood's greatest directors, was in charge of filming. Murphy played Lancaster's brother, and in such distinguished company he turned in the finest performance of his career.

Other excellent Westerns of 1960 included *The Magnificent Seven* and John Wayne's *North to Alaska*. The best Western of the next year also starred the Duke, in *The Comancheros*. Described in the previous chapter, *The Comancheros* was an outstanding film about Texas Rangers.

During the early 1960s NBC and ABC offered reruns of *The Lone Ranger* on afternoon television. In 1966 a new version of the masked man and Tonto was made available to young audiences. On Saturday mornings CBS aired an animated rendition of *The Lone Ranger*. The cartoon adventures of *The Lone Ranger* continued for three years, leaving CBS in September 1969, although there was a 1980 revival as part of *The Tarzan/Lone Ranger Hour*.

An hour-long Ranger series with humans debuted on Thursday nights over NBC on September 16, 1965. *Laredo* centered around Company B of the Texas Rangers in post-Civil

Peter Brown co-starred as a deputy on the TV series Lawman *from 1960-1964. During the next two seasons he played Texas Ranger Chad Cooper on the hour-long* Laredo.

War Texas. The stories emphasized humor as well as action. The stars were Neville Brand, Peter Brown, William Smith, and Phil Carey. Brand played Reese Bennett, a former Union officer (Brand was a combat veteran of World War II) who had reached his forties when he joined the Rangers. Bennett's age was a constant source of humor to his younger comrades. Brown, who had co-starred on *Lawman* from 1958 through

Rest in Peace

Two key figures in *The Lone Ranger* radio program died during this period. The prolific writer Fran Striker was killed in an automobile accident in 1962. Striker had churned out 156 Lone Ranger scripts year after year, in addition to work on other radio shows. He also created comic strips, comic books, Lone Ranger novels, and two fifteen-chapter movie serials.

In 1965 Brace Beemer died at the age of sixty-two. An early announcer on *The Lone Ranger* radio show, Beemer then played the title role from 1941 until original programming ended in 1954. Although we had no idea what Brace Beemer looked like, those of us who grew up listening to *The Lone Ranger* had lost a trusted friend with a deep, resonant voice.

1962, played Chad Cooper, a native of Boston who had been a member of the Border Patrol during the Civil War. After gunrunners killed several of his fellow officers, Cooper joined the Texas Rangers to continue his search for these border criminals. The muscular William Smith played gunfighter Joe Riley, who pinned on a Texas Ranger badge for the immunity it might afford him from other lawmen who sought him for earlier offenses.

Phil Carey played Captain Edward Parmalee, who sent the fun-loving trio on various assignments. A stern Ranger leader, Captain Parmalee was annoyed by their horseplay and constant jokes. A new Ranger, played by Robert Wolders, joined Company B during the second season. *Laredo* moved to Friday nights for its second year.

The second year was the last, and *Laredo* left the air in September 1967. By the late 1960s Western series, which had saturated TV screens for years, were falling out of favor with audiences. But *Laredo* was an entertaining series, packed with light-hearted action and boisterous stars. In 1968, only a year after the series ended, a 97-minute TV movie reprised *Laredo*'s characters and raucous adventures. *Three Guns For Texas* was edited from three episodes of *Laredo*. In addition to the stars of *Laredo*, *Three Guns For Texas* featured such familiar actors as Martin Milner, Albert Salmi, and Dub Taylor. *Three Guns For Texas* was a solid reminder of a lively, entertaining Ranger series.

In 1967 Warren Beatty and Faye Dunaway starred in *Bonnie and Clyde*, a fast-paced and stylish account of a Texas couple who were Depression era outlaws. Speeding from state to state in stolen cars, they robbed banks and killed a number of citizens, including several peace officers. In 1934 Captain

Frank Hamer, aided by five other lawmen, intercepted Bonnie and Clyde in their car in Louisiana. As Hamer approached the car, the outlaws scrambled for their guns. Hamer and the other officers opened fire, and Bonnie and Clyde died in the bullet-riddled automobile. The criminal odyssey of Bonnie and Clyde is greatly romanticized in the movie. A popular hit, *Bonnie and Clyde* received several Academy Award nominations.

Captain Frank Hamer was played by Denver Pyle. The veteran character actor was a physical match for Hamer in 1934—tall, heavyset and middleaged (Hamer was fifty). But he sported a sweeping handlebar mustache. Thin mustaches were popular during the 1930s, but handlebars were obsolete, and Hamer was clean-shaven.

Captain Hamer first appears onscreen stealthily approaching five members of the Barrow Gang in a car parked beside a stream in Missouri. He does not see Clyde Barrow, who shoots the gun from the Ranger's hand (just like Charles Starrett or the Lone Ranger would!). Hamer's hands are shackled with his own cuffs, and the fugitives pose with the captured prey for photographs which will be sent to newspapers. When Bonnie kisses Hamer on the lips, the offended lawman spits in her face. Enraged, Clyde throws the manacled Hamer into the water, nearly drowns him, then dumps him into a rowboat and lets him float away. This incident presumably fills Hamer with the burning determination to avenge his humiliation and kill Bonnie and Clyde.

In two subsequent scenes Captain Hamer learns the whereabouts of his prey and arranges the ambush. In the movie's final scene the officers blaze away from concealment, and Bonnie and Clyde are shot to pieces without warning. Captain Hamer had died in 1955, but his widow, Gladys, and Frank,

Jr., sued the producers of *Bonnie and Clyde* for defamation of character. It was inconceivable that Captain Frank Hamer could have been disarmed and handcuffed! Actually, in 1934 Bonnie and Clyde killed a constable in Commerce, Oklahoma,

In Bonnie and Clyde *the fugitives capture Ranger Captain Frank Hamer. Wearing the Ranger's hat, Bonnie (Faye Dunaway) kisses an indignant Hamer (Denver Pyle) while Clyde (Warren Beatty) enjoys the farce.*

then kidnapped his partner, not releasing the policeman until fourteen hours later. But the Commerce cop should not have been presented on movie screens as one of the most intrepid of all Texas Ranger captains. In 1971 the Hamer family received an out of court settlement.

In 1968 the Homer Garrison Texas Ranger Museum opened in Waco. The Texas Ranger Hall of Fame was added in 1976, with further additions in 1978 and the 1980s. Curator Gaines de Graffenreid assembled an impressive array of artifacts, including an exceptional firearms collection. A celebrated tourist destination, the Texas Ranger Hall of Fame and Museum also houses an excellent research facility, the Moody Texas Ranger Memorial Library. The lasting popularity of the Texas Ranger Hall of Fame and Museum underscores its significance as an institutional reflection of the Ranger mystique.

In 1969 six-foot-six Clint Walker played a Texas Ranger in a Western comedy, *The Great Bank Robbery*. The towering Walker earned fame in the title role of *Cheyenne*, a Warner Brothers TV Western that aired over ABC from 1955 through 1963. Walker starred with blond Kim Novak and comic actor Zero Mostel in *The Great Train Robbery*, which also featured such well-known character actors as Akim Tamiroff, Claude Akins, Sam Jaffe, John Anderson, Larry Storch, and Elisha Cook, Jr.

The story centers around a fortress of a bank, so impregnable that the ill-gotten gains of Jesse James and other bandits are deposited there for safe-keeping. But such a fortune attracts a varied host of greedy criminals. Mostel and Novak, masquerading as a preacher and his daughter, mastermind an elaborate robbery scheme. Tamiroff commands an army of

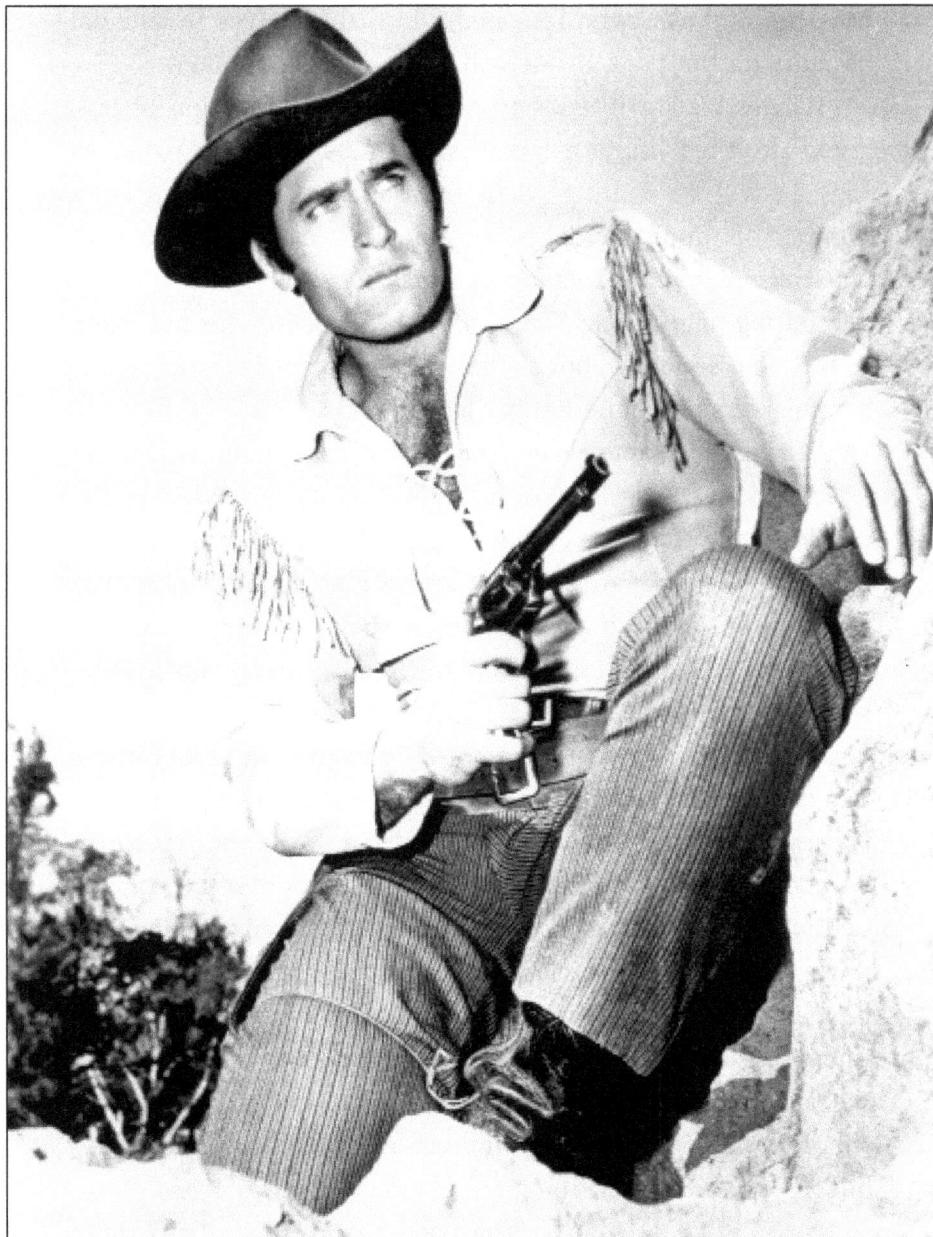

Big Clint Walker, who became a star on the TV series, Cheyenne, *played a Texas Ranger on the big screen in the comic Western* The Great Train Robbery.

Mexican outlaws, who repeatedly hurl themselves in suicidal assaults on the bank. Anderson is the crooked banker.

Ranger Walker intends to capture this aggregation of outlaws. He hires Chinese laborers to tunnel into the bank, so that he will be waiting when the outlaws break in. After a number of funny incidents, the movie climaxes with a wild chase scene involving galloping horsemen and speeding trains and daring balloonists. *The Great Train Robbery* was not made to be taken seriously, but the tall, slow-spoken Texas Ranger is a comic version of the Ranger legend.

During the same year *True Grit* earned John Wayne an Academy Award as Best Actor of 1969. As discussed in the previous chapter, Glen Campbell played a Texas Ranger in this memorable film. Although Campbell's performance was clumsy, the featured presence of a sharpshooting Ranger in such a prestigious film placed the Ranger image on a large stage.

Also in 1969 there was another comedy film about Texas Rangers, *The Over-the-Hill Gang*. Retired Ranger Captain Oran Hayes, played by sixty-nine-year-old Pat O'Brien, travels to Boulder, Nevada, to visit his daughter and son-in-law, played by Ricky and Kris Nelson, both still in their twenties. The captain's son-in-law was a crusading newspaperman who was running against Boulder's corrupt mayor, played with smiling nastiness by Edward Andrews. The mayor was backed by a crooked judge, sixty-four-year-old Andy Devine, and a fast-shooting sheriff, Jack Elam, who was a relatively youthful fifty-one.

Pat O'Brien telegraphs the code word "Brazos" to three members of his old Ranger company: seventy-five-year-old Walter Brennan, a retired sergeant living with his daughter in

Walter Brennan starred as a retired Ranger sergeant in The Over-the-Hill Gang *and* The Over-the-Hill Gang Rides Again.

Texas; sixty-six-year-old Chill Wills, a slick-fingered gambler in Abilene; and sixty-six-year-old Edgar Buchanan, residing in a retirement home in Kansas City. These three Western veterans, as well as O'Brien, all looked even older than their actual ages. "Time's been tailin' us and it's overtook us," observed Sergeant Brennan.

But the old geezers remembered their Ranger background. "No fella in the wrong can stand up agin' a fella that's in the right and keeps on a'comin'," Brennan reminded his three former comrades. He also added, "There's around 275 years of fightin' savvy in this room put all together in a lump." No longer fast on the draw, the retired Rangers plot to use their experience and the Ranger mystique. "Texas Rangers!" worriedly exclaims Andy Devine. "They're a mean bunch."

Aided by saloon owner Cassie McGuire, played by Gypsy Rose Lee, still vivacious at fifty-five, the Over-the-Hill Gang launches a series of ruses which divide and conquer the bad guys. The final triumph occurs at high noon in the "Gunfight at Cassie's Corral." After Ricky Nelson is sworn in as mayor, the geezers depart, proudly proclaiming: "No Ranger retires perpendicular!"

The Over-the-Hill Gang was silly but fast-paced, and it was fun to watch the old pros onscreen again. Sadly, both Pat O'Brien and Gypsy Rose Lee would die the next year. But response to *The Over-the-Hill Gang* was so good that producers Danny Thomas and Aaron Spelling came back in 1970 with *The Over-the-Hill Gang Rides Again*.

The opening scene was a spoof of the memorable opening of the 1969 hit *Butch Cassidy and the Sundance Kid*. Walter Brennan walks into a saloon where Chill Wills is accused of cheating by another gambler. "I wasn't cheatin'," insists Wills.

Brennan tries unsuccessfully to soothe the disagreement. "He called me a cheater!" growls Wills.

"Just tell my friend he ain't no cheater," pleads Brennan.

"No."

Brennan shrugs. "I'm afraid I just can't help you—Wyatt!"

Assuming that Chill Wills is Wyatt Earp, the gambler foresees doom. "I can't draw agin' you—you'd kill me."

The gambler quickly recants his insult, but as Wills and Brennan leave the saloon, he asks, "Your draw really as fast as they say?"

Wills stops. "You want to see it?" After an imperceptible hand motion, he queries, "You want to see it again?"

Brennan informs Wills that he has learned that another old Ranger comrade, the Baltimore Kid, is in trouble at Waco. They round up Edgar Buchanan from his retirement home, then head for Waco. (The town set had doubled as "Boulder" in the first Over-the-Hill Gang film, and it long had served as "Virginia City" in *Bonanza*.) In Waco they are reacquainted with Andy Devine, now a newspaperman who had notified them about the Baltimore Kid. They find that the Kid is now a drunken bum.

The Baltimore Kid is played by seventy-one-year-old Fred Astaire. He is sobered up by his three Ranger buddies, who also outfit him and publicize his heroic past. Soon the Baltimore Kid is appointed city marshal of Waco, and the three retired Rangers serve as his deputies. They vanquish the bad guys, then fake the death of the Baltimore Kid, so that his reputation will attract no more gunfighters. But the novelty had worn off the Ranger oldtimers, and there were no more Over-the-Hill Gang sequels.

The Over-the-Hill Gang Rides Again is an appropriate be-

ginning to Ranger entertainment during the 1970s. Only a handful of motion pictures featured Texas Rangers during the decade, and there were no Ranger series on television. Entertainment focusing on Texas Rangers seemed decidedly "over-the-hill" during the 1970s.

In 1974 Goldie Hawn and Ben Johnson starred in *The Sugarland Express*, based on factual events in southeast Texas. In a desperate effort to save her little boy from adoption, Goldie helps her husband escape from prison. The couple hijacks a Highway Patrol car and abducts a State Policeman. Texas Ranger Ben Johnson directs the pursuit, and finally a Ranger marksman shoots Goldie's husband to death. The movie was popular, but the most notable aspect of *The Sugarland Express* is that it is the first feature film directed by Steven Spielberg.

Two years later Ben Johnson starred in another motion picture with a Ranger connection and based on real crimes. In 1946 a series of murders terrified Texarkana, and the crime spree was never solved. The story was loosely related in *The Town That Dreaded Sundown*, but the film was mediocre and did little to perpetuate the Ranger mystique.

Also in 1976 there was a Ranger presence in a highly successful Clint Eastwood movie, *The Outlaw Josey Wales*. Eastwood starred as the title character, a Missouri farmer during the Civil War whose family is murdered and his home is burned by Kansas Redlegs. Seeking vengeance, Wales joins the guerrilla raiders of Bloody Bill Anderson. Refusing to surrender at the end of the war, Wales is branded an outlaw with a $5,000 price on his head. He flees south, and the latter half of the story takes place in Texas (the movie actually was filmed in Utah and northern California). Along the way a variety of

Clint Eastwood directed and starred in Outlaw Josey Wales, *which included a Ranger scene and which was one of the few hit Westerns of the 1970s.*

travelers attach themselves to Wales, and there are violent encounters with Redleg pursuers, bounty hunters, Comanches and others foolish enough to challenge the *pistolero*.

Josey Wales sadly remarks to a companion, played with wry humor by Chief Dan George, "When I get to liking someone they ain't around long." Chief Dan George replies, "I notice when you get to *dis*liking someone they ain't around for long neither."

At the end of a long and murderous tale, two Texas Rangers ride into the little town of Santo Rio in search of Josey Wales. But Wales has defended the townspeople, and with the outlaw present they swear an affidavit that they saw him killed. The Rangers leave with the document, saying that they will not return. "Must be five thousand men and women in Texas right now," remarks one tall, imposing Ranger. "Can't get 'em all."

The Outlaw Josey Wales was one of the few Western hits of the decade. Before he directed and starred in the film, Eastwood was aware that Hollywood regarded Westerns as "financial leprosy." Despite the success of this 1976 motion picture, there were no other films during the 1970s, on large or small screens, which featured Texas Rangers.

1960s and 1970s

BEST RANGER MOVIES
The Comancheros (1961—John Wayne)
True Grit (1969—John Wayne)

BEST RANGER TV SERIES
Laredo (1965-1967—Neville Brand, Peter Brown,
William Smith, Phil Carey)

BEST RANGER BOOKS
True Grit (1968—Charles Portis)
"I'm Frank Hamer" (1968—H. Gordon Frost
and John H. Jenkins)

BEST NEW TEXAS RANGER MUSEUM
The Homer Garrison Texas Ranger Museum
(1968—Waco)

BEST NEW MAJOR LEAGUE BASEBALL TEAM NICKNAME
The Texas Rangers (1972)

R.I.P.
Captain M.T. "Lone Wolf" Gonzaullas, 85 (1977)

RANGER EVENTS
In 1962 Col. Homer Garrison announced that the official Texas Ranger badge would become the traditional "wagon wheel" badge, the star within a circle carved from a Mexican silver coin by many old-time Rangers.

After three decades of supervising the Rangers, Homer Garrison died in 1968. His successor, Col. Wilson E. Speir, accelerated training programs and upgraded equipment. The force was increased from 62 to 73 in 1969, then to 82 in 1971, 88 in 1974 and 94 in 1975.

1980s: Lonesome Dove

"Me and you done our work too well. We killed off most of the people that made this country interesting to begin with."
—Gus McCrae to Woodrow Call,
former Ranger captains in *Lonesome Dove*

During the 1980s relatively few Western movies were filmed in comparison with previous decades. Western novels declined markedly in popularity, and fresh Western material— as opposed to old movies and reruns of former weekly series—seldom appeared on television. Nevertheless, a few notable motion pictures and TV movies featured Texas Rangers. And an extraordinary novel, *Lonesome Dove*, was centered around two memorable ex-Rangers. Before the decade ended, *Lonesome Dove* was transformed into one of the most successful mini-series in television history. Therefore the 1980s, in quality if not in quantity, produced a Ranger renaissance in popular culture.

In 1981, after a twenty-three-year absence from the big screen, the Lone Ranger and Silver galloped back onto motion picture screens. *The Legend of the Lone Ranger* provided the most detailed portrayal of the Lone Ranger's early life ever presented on film, TV, or radio. Indeed, some of these details had never before been part of the familiar story.

The Legend of the Lone Ranger begins in Texas in 1854,

An unknown actor, Klinton Spilsbury, starred in The Legend of the Lone Ranger.

with masked raiders galloping through the countryside. Young Johnny Reid saves an Indian boy named Tonto. But shortly afterward the raiders strike the Reid ranch and murder Johnny's parents. Tonto takes Johnny to his tribe, where his new friend is raised as an Indian and taught "what is just and which trail to follow—the trail of justice." Tonto and Johnny become blood brothers in a ceremony. Finally Dan Reid discovers his little brother among the Indians. Johnny is sent to live with an aunt in Detroit, where he will receive an education.

As a young attorney, John Reid returns to Texas, traveling by stagecoach to Del Rio, where his brother Dan is now a captain of Rangers. On the stagecoach he meets a pretty young woman, Amy Striker, who intends to write for her uncle's Del Rio newspaper. (Fran Striker, prolific writer of Lone Ranger scripts, apparently was the inspiration for this new character.) John Reid helps save the stagecoach from an outlaw attack, and later, in Del Rio, John and Amy kiss—certainly a fresh adventure for the Lone Ranger!

Amy's uncle is an outspoken critic of the Butch Cavendish Gang. After the uncle is murdered, John Reid rides with Texas Rangers in pursuit. The familiar canyon ambush is executed by a small army of outlaws, armed with rifles and a Gatling gun and commanded by Major Bartholomew ("Butch") Cavendish. Tonto happens upon the fallen Rangers and discovers his boyhood friend. Taken back to Tonto's tribe, Reid recovers, tames a white stallion, and practices with six-guns. Tonto presents him with a silver bullet.

"Tribal chiefs first used silver on their arrows," points out Tonto. "Makes 'em fly longer and faster. Silver is pure. It's been a symbol of justice and purity since the year of the sun."

All of this takes up half of the movie. Donning a mask to

Farewell, Faithful Companion

Jay Silverheels played Tonto, faithful companion to the Lone Ranger, in every episode of the television series, 1949-1957. Clad in buckskin and headband, and riding his paint horse Scout, Tonto also supported the most famous of all Rangers in two feature films, *The Lone Ranger* (1956) and *The Lone Ranger and the Lost City of Gold* (1958).

A heavy smoker, Silverheels suffered a heart attack during a fight scene for television, and Tonto had to be written out of the series until the actor recovered. Like Clayton Moore, when the TV series ended Silverheels made frequent public appearances in the role that had brought him fame. His show featured Native American culture, and occasionally Silverheels appeared alongside Moore. He also engaged in professional harness racing, winning a number of events.

Unlike Clayton Moore, Silverheels continued his movie career after the close of the series. His last role was in a Glenn Ford Western, *Santee* (1973). In 1974 Silverheels suffered a stroke, and his health steadily declined. John Todd, who played Tonto on the radio for more than two decades, had died in 1957 at the age of eighty. On March 5, 1980, sixty-two-year-old Jay Silverheels died in the Motion Picture and Television Home and Hospital in California. His ashes were scattered over Canada's Six Nations Reservation where he was born.

prevent the outlaws from learning his identity, Reid goes after Cavendish—accompanied by Tonto, who has no intention of living on a reservation. Cavendish, as a Civil War major, was courtmartialed, and the document was signed by General U.S. Grant. President Grant is now on a train headed for Del Rio and a wild game hunt. Also in the hunting party are Buffalo Bill Cody, Wild Bill Hickok, and George Armstrong Custer. The presidential car is detached from the train, and President Grant is spirited to the fortified hideout of Cavendish, who intends to force the President to sign a document separating Texas from the United States. Cavendish is determined to rule over Texas. But the Lone Ranger and Tonto rescue President Grant, while the hideout is stormed by Custer, Wild Bill, Buffalo Bill, and the U.S. Cavalry.

The action was punctuated with considerable violence and a great deal of profanity. Brian Garfield commented that "this rehash of the old radio show is too violent and gory for tykes and too stupid for grown-ups." Another problem was the lead actors. Michael Horse was bland as Tonto, and the unknown Klinton Spilsbury proved so inept that his voice was dubbed by actor James Keach. But Lone Ranger fans could enjoy the closing credits, with the old radio recording—"With his friend Tonto, the daring and resourceful masked rider of the plains led the fight for law and order in the early Western United States. Nowhere in the pages of history can one find a greater champion of justice. The Lone Ranger rides again!"—pronounced with the William Tell Overture throbbing in the background.

In 1982 an excellent TV movie appeared on PBS, funded by the National Endowment For The Humanities and the Corporation For Public Broadcasting. *The Ballad of Gregorio Cortez* was based on a 1958 non-fiction book by Americo

Paredes, *With His Pistol in His Hand: A Border Ballad And Its Hero.* Gregorio Cortez was born in Mexico in 1876, then moved with his family to south Texas when he was twelve. He worked as a *vaquero*, but never learned to speak English. In 1901 the sheriff of Karnes County, who spoke no Spanish, came to the Cortez home to investigate a reported horse theft. The sheriff brought a deputy as interpreter, but he botched the translation. The misunderstanding angered the sheriff, who drew a gun and mortally wounded Gregorio's brother. Gregorio shot the sheriff to death, then escaped.

A massive manhunt ensued, led by Texas Rangers and other officers, and including as many as 300 possemen, who were attracted by a reward of $1,000. Early in the pursuit another sheriff was killed, along with a posseman who was slain by friendly fire. Cortez's wife and four children were thrown in jail. But for eleven days Cortez eluded capture, riding more than 400 miles and hiking another 120 miles.

After Cortez finally was captured, his court-appointed lawyer learned of the confused translation. Cortez was tried seven times over a four-year period. Eventually he was acquitted of murdering the sheriff of Karnes County and the posseman, but he was convicted of murdering the second sheriff and stealing a horse during the fight. Sentenced to life imprisonment, Cortez was pardoned by the governor in 1913, but he died three years later.

Beginning with his flight against great odds, Gregorio Cortez became a hero to the Tejanos of south Texas, who long had suffered racial prejudice. Texas Rangers were especially feared by Tejanos and border Mexicans. Tejanos contributed to the legal fund of Cortez, while a new ballad, *El Corrido de Gregorio Cortez*, was widely performed and enjoyed.

Edward James Olmos starred in the title role of *The Ballad of Gregorio Cortez*. Speaking in Spanish throughout the film, Olmos artfully reflected fear, courage, grief and anger. Also turning in excellent performances were James Gammon, as a sheriff who saves Cortez from a lynch mob, and Barry Corbin as the defense attorney. Brian James played Texas Ranger Captain J. H. Rogers with quiet authority.

Captain Rogers directed the manhunt, and following the capture of Cortez he was feted at a congratulatory dinner. It was remarked that Gregorio Cortez had extended the life of the Texas Rangers. There had been recent talk of abolishing the seemingly old-fashioned Rangers, but during the pursuit Captain Rogers ably utilized such modern technology as telephones, trains and telegraphs. "It's a new century," he explained at the dinner. "We gotta be a new type of law enforcement agency right along with it. Things are changin' fast."

The following year a Ranger movie anticipated a major TV series of the next decade. In 1983 action hero Chuck Norris starred as *Lone Wolf McQuade*, a contemporary Texas Ranger stationed in El Paso. Norris was a six-time world middleweight karate champ who turned to acting during the 1970s. After utilizing war movies and crime dramas to showcase his martial arts skills, Norris found the role of a Texas Ranger a natural career move. One of the most famous of all twentieth century Rangers was Captain M. T. "Lone Wolf" Gonzaullas, so Chuck Norris portrayed J. J. "Lone Wolf" McQuade. Over the opening and closing credits a lone wolf loped around symbolically, and Ranger McQuade owned a wolf-like dog.

Ranger McQuade sports a full beard and wears his badge on an unbuttoned double-breasted shirt. McQuade swills beer and lives in a pigsty. He works alone and rebels against

An excellent TV movie, The Ballad of Gregorio Cortez, *related the tragedy involving Cortez and the massive manhunt ked by the Texas Rangers.*

bureaucratic authority, represented by his Ranger captain in El Paso. A former marine, McQuade is an expert shot with his Magnum revolver, but he often leaves his gun holstered to make arrests by pummeling various bad guys with his martial arts expertise.

The movie opens with Mexican horse rustlers intercepted at the border by deputy sheriffs and DPS patrolmen. After a shootout the lawmen are surrounded, but when they are about to be executed, Lone Wolf McQuade charges to the rescue.

"Ain't no one ever killed no Texas Ranger and lived to tell it," warns one of the rustlers. Ranger McQuade shoots and batters the rustlers, then faces the leader. "You know," challenges the chief rustler, "once a Texas Ranger kicked my father's teeth out. Would you do that to me, Texas Ranger?" An instant later Ranger McQuade kicks his teeth out.

McQuade soon encounters a more formidable bad guy, Rawley Wilkes, played with smiling evil by David Carradine, a

Chuck Norris played a scruffy Texas Ranger in Lone Wolf McQuade, *forerunner of his popular TV series a decade later.*

martial arts expert in real life. Wilkes is a drug dealer who has a secret base in Mexico. He hijacks a military truckload of weapons, intending to sell them to terrorists and Latin American drug kings. Wilkes' henchmen kidnap McQuade's daughter (he is divorced), kill her boyfriend, and shoot McQuade's dog. McQuade's best friend, a retired Ranger played by the colorful L. Q. Jones, also is killed by Wilkes' men. And McQuade's girlfriend, played by beautiful Barbara Carrera, is killed by Wilkes. Wilkes nearly kills McQuade, and tears his badge from his shirt. "Something to remember you by," smirks Wilkes. "Adios."

Ranger McQuade survives to assault Wilkes' base in Mexico. Aided by a couple of other officers, McQuade blows up the base, destroys the gang, then, following a rousing martial arts battle, kills Wilkes. Proudly wearing his badge again, McQuade is honored before a large crowd—including his daughter and ex-wife—in El Paso.

Unlike most Ranger films, *Lone Wolf McQuade* was shot on location in Texas. But the characters were one-dimensional, even cartoonish, and after McQuade established his invincibility in the opening scene, no doubt remained that he would triumph over the bad guys. Nevertheless, *Lone Wolf McQuade* was one Chuck Norris' most successful films. Gradually eclipsed in action movies by Arnold Schwarzenegger, Sylvester Stallone, Steven Seagal and Jean-Claude Van Damme, Norris turned to television. Ten years after *Lone Wolf McQuade*, Chuck Norris would explode on the nation's small screens with a hit series, *Walker, Texas Ranger*.

In 1986, the year of the Texas Sesquicentennial, native Texan Willie Nelson played a Ranger on the popular crime series, *Miami Vice*. A Country Music icon, Nelson was entirely

Famed singer Willie Nelson was featured in a 1986 episode of Miami Vice *as a Texas Ranger. A few years later Willie co-starred in two Ranger movies on TV,* A Pair of Aces *and* Another Pair of Aces.

convincing as an old Ranger who had pursued vicious drug dealers to Miami to avenge the death of his partner in Texas. Employing an old-fashioned Colt .45 revolver, he aids Don Johnson and the other vice detectives. Although already wounded, Nelson engages in the climactic shootout with his Ranger badge proudly pinned to his shirt and a Western hat atop his head. Willie and the vice cops wipe out the drug gang, but again he is shot. In the best Ranger tradition, Willie Nelson dies a hero.

Also in 1986 *The Texas Chainsaw Massacre 2* starred Dennis Hopper as an ex-Ranger. In 1974 *The Texas Chainsaw Massacre* helped launch the blood and gore genre, as teenagers are attacked by a maniacal, cannibalistic family with power tools. *The Texas Chainsaw Massacre* unaccountably became a cult classic, and the first of three sequels was released in 1986. But Hopper's ex-Ranger is almost as depraved as the murderous family he pursues. *The Texas Chainsaw Massacre 2*, therefore, is no more important to Ranger films than *Jesse James Meets Frankenstein's Daughter* or *Billy the Kid vs. Dracula* were to gunfighter movies.

Perhaps the most convincing cinematic portrayal of a contemporary Texas Ranger was turned in by Nick Nolte in *Extreme Prejudice*, a 1987 film set along the border. A former football player, Nolte brought a strong and imposing physique to the role of Jack Benteen, a third-generation Ranger. Nolte presented the right look with a long-sleeved shirt and tie, Western hat, and gun rig for his heavy automatic. The wagon wheel badge was conspicuous on his shirt front.

Native Texan Powers Boothe radiates danger as Cash Bailey, Benteen's best friend while they were schoolboys. Now Bailey runs cocaine into Texas from Mexico. When he tries to

bribe his old Buddy, Benteen grunts in best Ranger fashion, "You can't buy the badge,"

Another Texan, Rip Torn, plays a likeable but doomed sheriff who is Benteen's mentor. Remarking on a current Ranger issue, Benteen tells the sheriff that he expects to hear him continue to complain about the legislature admitting females to the Rangers. "Hell, I don't care, as long as she's six-foot-six, mean as a snake. State Legislature!" snorts the sheriff. "Shit, Jack, the only thing worse than a politician is a child molester."

(A similar sentiment about the lawman's contempt for politicians is expressed by Ranger Captain Dan Reid in *Legend of the Lone Ranger*: "In Texas, robbers are outlaws. In Washington, robbers are elected.")

The film opens with Ranger Benteen reluctantly forced to kill a coke runner. As Benteen's lethal adventures mount, one bad guy observes with grudging admiration, "That Ranger, there, that's one crazy mother."

Plot complications include a para-military group planning to steal a vast amount of Bailey's cash, and Bailey's abduction into Mexico of his former sweetheart—who currently is Ranger Benteen's sweetheart. Benteen slips into Mexico to rescue her and to have it out with his former buddy. The para-military group is present, and when the shooting starts, the final scene becomes an updated version of the closing shootout of *The Wild Bunch*.

Filled with action, conflict, and boasting a stalwart, believable hero, *Extreme Prejudice* is an entertaining motion picture. As Jack Benteen, Nick Nolte creates the personification of a tough, courageous Texas Ranger. Nolte benefited from the project's technical advisor, Texas Ranger Joaquin Jackson. There has never been a more powerful version of a Ranger.

The 1980s closed with an epic television mini-series cen-tered around three memorable ex-Rangers. Airing in 1989, *Lonesome Dove* mesmerized viewing audiences with the adven-

Radiating quiet power, Nick Nolte played a rugged contemporary Ranger in Extreme Prejudice.

Robert Duvall and Texan Tommy Lee Jones starred as grizzled former Texas Rangers Gus McCrae and Woodrow Call in the blockbuster TV miniseries, Lonesome Dove.

tures of Gus McCrae and Woodrow Call. During the 1970s
Texas author Larry McMurtry had conceived the project of famous old Rangers trailing a cattle herd to Montana. The author of this book was present when McMurtry discussed his
new project at a summer lecture series at the University of
Texas at Austin. McMurtry developed *Lonesome Dove* with a
movie in mind. He hoped that the three former Rangers—
McCrae, Call and ill-fated Jake Spoon—would be played by
James Stewart, John Wayne and Henry Fonda, and these stars
influenced the creation of his characters.

McMurtry's long, magnificent novel was published in
1985, and the best-seller won the Pulitzer Prize. Because of its
length, *Lonesome Dove* was better suited to a TV mini-series
than to the comparative brevity of a motion picture. But by the
time *Lonesome Dove* was filmed, John Wayne and Henry Fonda
had been dead for years, and James Stewart was elderly.
Nevertheless, a superb cast was assembled: Robert Duvall delivered a masterful performance as romantic, adventurous,
garrulous Gus; Texan Tommy Lee Jones was indefatigable and
explosive as Captain Call; Angelica Huston was a tower of fem-
inine strength as Clara, Gus' lost love; lovely Diane Lane as
Lorie, big Robert Urich as Spoon, likeable Danny Glover as
Deets, young Rick Schroder as Newt, and a host of others
brought life to a rich assemblage of characters.

Gus and Call were famous Texas Rangers who for two
decades had played a leading role in making the Lone Star State
safe from bandits and Comanches. "Me and you done our work
too well," remarked Gus to Call. "We killed off most of the people that made this country interesting to begin with."

As proprietors of the Hat Creek Cattle Company at tiny
Lonesome Dove, the retired Rangers restlessly pursue another

frontier adventure in 1876, driving a herd of cattle north to establish a ranch in Montana. In San Antonio Gus pistol-whips an insolent bartender in the Buckhorn Saloon. "He enjoyed having been a famous Texas Ranger," reflected Call, "and was often put out if he didn't receive all the praise he had coming."

During the long drive to Montana, the Texans encounter an assortment of murderous frontier riffraff. Call and Gus revert to their Ranger creed, tracking and killing the worst of the killers. They are forced to hang their old comrade, Jake Spoon, who had fallen in with a vicious gang (Jake spurred his horse from underneath himself, so that Gus would not have to use his quirt). Gus happily romances both Lorie and Clara, but always presses onward. "I'd like to see at least one more place that ain't settled before I take up the rockin' chair."

But in Montana Gus takes two arrows in the leg from Sioux warriors. Although he successfully fights off the party, his leg is amputated. Blood poisoning has set in, however, and the most charming character in the film dies. Gus extracts a deathbed promise from Call to bury him at a spot in Texas where he had picnicked with Clara. Call resolutely hauls the corpse from Montana to Texas, overcoming all manner of hardships. (Cattle baron Charles Goodnight, a former Texas Ranger, faced a similar situation in 1867, when his partner, Oliver Loving, caught two arrows in his arm while traversing the Goodnight-Loving Trail. Loving fought off the warriors, but his arm was amputated by a New Mexico military surgeon. On his deathbed he asked Goodnight to bury him near his home in Weatherford. Goodnight and the corpse were accompanied back to Texas by more than seventy riders. McMurtry adapted and expanded the Goodnight-Loving incident for Gus and Call.)

Dramatic, witty, exciting, romantic, tragic, and beautifully

filmed, *Lonesome Dove* was a superlative entertainment. The public had fallen in love with the two old Rangers, and it seemed inevitable that there would be sequels and prequels during the 1990s.

1980S

BEST RANGER MOVIE
Extreme Prejudice (1987—Nick Nolte)

BEST RANGER TV MOVIE
The Ballad of Gregorio Cortez
(1982—Edward James Olmos)

BEST RANGER TV MINI-SERIES
Lonesome Dove (1989—Robert Duvall
and Tommy Lee Jones)

BEST RANGER BOOKS
Lonesome Dove (1985—Larry McMurtry)
Texas (1985—James Michener)
Lone Wolf (1980—Brownson Malsch)

RANGER EVENTS
The Ranger force was equipped with up-to-date weaponry, speedy automobiles, and sophisticated communications and crime detection equipment. Training was intensified, but Ranger pay increases were provided, along with hospitalization, a paid life insurance policy, and other benefits. A long list of applicants testified to the elite status of the Texas Rangers.

1990s: Walker, Texas Ranger

"Well, bein' a Ranger means you can die any day. You don't want to risk it, you oughta quit."
—Woodrow Call to Gus McCrae in *Dead Man's Walk*

The return of Texas Rangers to popular culture that began in the 1980s continued strongly during the 1990s. There were numerous TV movies and mini-series, along with a popular weekly series. Several motion pictures included Rangers, and Larry McMurtry penned three more novels with further adventures of Woodrow Call and Gus McCrae.

In 1990 a good-natured TV movie, *A Pair of Aces*, starred Kris Kristofferson as Texas Ranger Captain Rip Metcalf and Willie Nelson as Billy Roy. Rip Torn, a native Texan like Kristofferson and Nelson, was featured as Ranger Captain Jack Parsons. On the trail of a serial killer, Captain Metcalf is saddled with Billy Roy, a talktative safecracker who is in his custody. Kristofferson and Nelson, pals in real life, made a delightful buddy team, reminiscent of Gus McCrae and Woodrow Call. The film was shot on location in Austin.

A Pair of Aces was well-received, and the next year Kristofferson and Nelson happily teamed in *Another Pair of Aces: Three of a Kind*. Rip Torn also returned, and beautiful

146

Texan Kris Kristofferson co-starred with his pal, Willie Nelson, as a Texas Ranger in A Pair of Aces *and* Another Pair of Aces.

Joan Severance was added to the cast. Indeed, scenes regarded as too sexy for television were added to the video. When not distracted by Severance, the stars worked to clear a fellow Ranger of a murder charge.

In 1993 powerhouse actors Clint Eastwood and Kevin Costner co-starred in *A Perfect World*, which Eastwood directed. Eastwood played 1960s Texas Ranger Red Garnet. While Garnet was county sheriff at Amarillo, he dealt with Butch Haynes, a juvenile delinquent played by Costner. By 1963 Butch has become a murderer who escapes from prison

Clint Eastwood as Ranger Captain Red Garnet in A Perfect World.

and heads for the Texas Panhandle, where "there are more roads than people." After abducting an eight-year-old boy, played with innocent charm by J. J. Lowther, Butch kills his fellow escapee. Butch and the boy, who is hungry for a father figure, develops a bond while they drive northward in stolen cars.

Pursuit efforts are led by Ranger Garnet, who is headquartered in Austin. Governor John Connally allows the Rangers to use his new trailer, drawn by a DPS pickup, as a command vehicle. The trailer is equipped with radios—and T-bone steaks—and is about to be used by the governor when he welcomes President Kennedy to Texas. Governor Connally informs reporters, "It's an amazing futuristic piece of law enforcement equipment."

In his command vehicle, Garnet has another Ranger and other officers, including a criminologist, Sally Gerber. Gerber is played with intelligence and a flawless Texas accent by the superb actress, Laura Dern. As Garnet, Eastwood is quiet-spoken, efficient and tough. With his rugged good looks and clad in a tie, sunglasses and Stetson, the tall actor resembles a Ranger recruiter. The Texas Rangers assisted with the movie, which was filmed in Austin and a variety of Hill Country locations. Costner's character is alternately laid-back and vicious, and the film's ending is depressing. But *A Perfect World* offers the authentic flavor of Texas and a positive image of modern Rangers.

The same Texas flavor and contemporary Ranger image was offered to TV audiences in 1993. A decade after he played Lone Wolf McQuade, Chuck Norris decided to bring another contemporary Ranger to television. The series, *Walker, Texas Ranger*, would be filmed at Las Colinas Studios, outside

of Dallas, and at locations in and around Dallas and Fort Worth. The character, Ranger Cordell Walker, retained many of the traits of J. J. McQuade: he was a maverick impatient of stifling regulations and bureaucrats; a throwback to the hardnosed methods of earlier years; a casual dresser who sported a beard and rangle clothes—in contrast to the clean-shaven, professional look of most contemporary Rangers. Also like McQuade, Walker was a master of martial arts and firearms.

Walker's father was a Cherokee from Oklahoma and his mother was an Anglo; as a boy he saw his parents fatally stabbed by racists. A Cherokee uncle lives at the ranch home of Ranger Walker, who was state champion bull rider five years earlier. In law enforcement, Walker is so indomitable that he is praised by an admirer in the opening episode as "the most famous Texas Ranger, alive or dead."

In the first episode Walker's young, clean-cut partner was killed by being too trusting, a quality that had been regarded as "dangerous for a Ranger." Walker's new partner, Jimmy Trivette, also is young and clean-cut. Trivette was a wide receiver at Penn State who played one season for the Dallas Cowboys before an injury ended his football career. Then he became a highway patrolman and, in fulfillment of a boyhood dream, a Texas Ranger. Trivette told Walker that as a kid growing up in Baltimore, "every Saturday morning I used to get up and sneak into my living room and watch my favorite TV show, about the most famous Texas Ranger of all time." Trivette's hero, of course, was the Lone Ranger. "Now here comes this guy on a white horse and he goes where he wants to go. He does what he wants to do. He's got the guts to say, there is right, there is wrong." Trivette dresses neatly, in coat and tie and Stetson. He is an expert with computers and mod-

ern law enforcement methods, but he also is skilled in martial arts.

Trivette was encouraged to enter law enforcement by a former Ranger named C. D. Parker, whose career was ended by a bullet in the knee. C. D.'s Bar and Grill, located in Fort Worth's Stockyards District, is a popular Ranger hangout, and C. D. is an old pal of Walker. During the early episodes C. D. was played by Gailard Sartain, who soon was replaced by native Texan Noble Willingham. James Drury, famous for his television role as *The Virginian*, was cast as Walker's Ranger captain. But a contract could not be agreed upon, and Drury left the show, returning to his home in Houston. Thereafter there was no captain; Walker was the ranking Ranger.

Another key role, beautiful Alex Cahill, was filled by blond Sheree J. Wilson. Cahill, as an assistant district attorney, headquartered in the Tarrant County Courthouse in downtown Fort Worth. Walker also had an office in the picturesque 1891 courthouse, and the

Chuck Norris starred in the popular TV series Walker, Texas Ranger *for eight seasons.*

Ranger and the lady D.A. enjoyed a mutual attraction. "Walker," smiled Alex after one of his many good deeds, "there's a special place in heaven for people like you." Another good deed brought a hug from Alex, and Walker said, "I could get used to that." He would have eight seasons to get used to that, and onscreen Walker and Alex became a familiar couple around Fort Worth.

Walker premiered in 1993 with an episode entitled "One Riot, One Ranger." The title referred to the legendary nineteenth century incident when a town mayor, facing anarchy, telegraphed frantically for Texas Rangers to come on the next train. At the depot a single Texas Ranger stepped off the train. The mayor, in dismay, asked where the other Rangers were. "There's only one riot," came the probably apocryphal reply. A bad guy in the initial episode of *Walker* expressed his concern about facing Texas Rangers. "They make up their own rules as they go. Worse than the FBI. 'One riot, one Ranger.' That's what their motto is."

In the opening scene of "One Riot, One Ranger," Walker chases four robbers across the border to a Mexican cantina. "This is Mexico, Ranger!" exclaims one robber. "You got no right!"

"I've got no right?" Walker knocks out the bad guy with his right hand. "I think that's a pretty good right!"

Walker kick-punches all four robbers into unconsciousness, then dumps them into the bed of his pickup (before making an arrest, he always drops the tailgate of his truck). Walker takes his prisoners back into Texas at a lonely border crossing where the guard is accustomed to his "cargo." The Ranger hauls his captives several hundred miles to Fort Worth, where Assistant D.A. Alex Cahill tells him the arrest was illegal and the pris-

oners must be released. But a phone call to the governor of Sonora reveals that Walker has a personal extradition agreement (of course, the Mexican State of Sonora adjoins Arizona, not Texas—a minor detail).

Having disposed of the Mexican thieves, Walker now concentrates on a gang of Fort Worth bank robbers who have just killed his partner. Although Walker has misgivings about his new partner, Jimmy Trivette, the young Ranger soon proves his worth. After taking time out to ride a bull, "Terminator," for a charitable event at the Coliseum in the Stockyards, Walker closes in on the gang. Aided by Trivette and C. D. (who, though retired, still wears his Ranger badge and packs a revolver), Walker thwarts the gang's attempt to rob four banks simultaneously in downtown Fort Worth.

As indicated by "One Riot, One Ranger," *Walker Texas Ranger* would feature sparse, simple dialogue and evil, one-dimensional criminals. Walker and his friends dispatched direct justice with shootouts and martial arts brawls. (Walker would never draw his revolver if there were any opportunity to kick-punch the bad guys.) The CBS action show was an immediate hit. Indeed, when production financing unexpectedly collapsed after three episodes, CBS promptly provided the backing necessary to keep *Walker* on the air.

Walker, Texas Ranger became the mainstay of CBS-TV's Saturday night lineup. Chuck Norris was immersed in every aspect of the show, and he was extremely proud of his production crew. Walker showcased such familiar guest stars as Barbara Mandrell, Ernest Borgnine, Dionne Warwick, Lee Majors, Mackenzie Phillips, Erik Estrada, and many others. U.S. Senator Kay Bailey Hutchison made an appearance in 1997, and a few years later Ann Jillian played a female sena-

Ranger Badges

Not until the Indian wars subsided in the mid-1870s were Texas Rangers regarded primarily as peace officers rather than as Indian fighters. Badges were not provided by the state, but many Rangers began carving their own—out of Mexican silver coins, or tin cans, or wood, or sometimes even leather. These badges always featured a star, often surrounded by a circle—the famous "wagon wheel badge," a natural design when cut from a coin. Some badges had a shield surrounding the star, or a shield with a star punched out of the center. "TEXAS RANGER" or "STATE RANGER" usually was cut into the badge. Often there was no clasp; Rangers frequently worked undercover and did not wear a badge, keeping it inside a pocket until it was necessary to reveal their identity. After 1935, when the Texas Rangers became part of the Department of Public Safety, Rangers began wearing the badge of the highway patrol. But in 1967 the DPS changed the Ranger badge to the traditional star within a circle.

The movies and TV provided an accurate reflection of the variety and tradition of Ranger badges. Like their real-life counterparts, many celluloid Rangers did not openly wear badges. Many others donned some sort of shield, with "RANGER" or "TEXAS RANGER" as a label. In the opening television episode of *The Lone Ranger*, the six Rangers each sport a star within a shield.

Another television Ranger, Cordell Walker, wore a badge which apparently was made of Kryptonite. In one episode of Walker, Texas Ranger, he is shot in the chest by a criminal. Tumbled backward by the impact, Walker clutches his chest as he falls. But no blood emerges, and Walker looks at his chest. His Ranger badge saved his life, suffering only a dent in the star from the high velocity bullet.

tor from Texas. The series began to utilize flashback sequences, with Norris playing frontier Ranger Hayes Cooper. A
theme song was developed: "In the eyes of a Ranger . . . Any
wrong you do he's gonna see/When you're in Texas look behind you/'Cause that's where the Ranger's gonna be."

The theme song introduced each episode. Norris, clad in a
hat and a long duster and sporting a steely glare, chanted the
lyrics. In one episode pretty Alex Cahill tells Walker, "Oh,
honey, you know I love you even though you can't sing."

But if Walker could not sing he certainly could perform a
variety of heroics. He once leaped from a helicopter into a lake
to rescue a bound girl. At the Mesquite Rodeo Arena Walker
rode a wild bronc, donating his $10,000 prize to a wildlife
charity—then immediately left the arena with his partner to
thwart an armored truck robbery. In a two-part 1994 episode
entitled, "Deadly Reunion," Walker defends his championship
in combat pistol competition with a perfect score. The title
refers to a Ranger Retiree Reunion in Fort Worth, and prominent among the retirees are L. Q. Jones and R. G. Armstrong,
who both had played alongside Norris in *Lone Wolf McQuade*.
Another featured character is former Ranger Stuart Whitman,
who played a reluctant Ranger recruit in *The Comancheros*,
and who died a hero's death in "Deadly Reunion."

Tourists to the Texas Ranger Hall of Fame and Museum in
Waco began to ask where Cordell Walker was stationed. In
1995 *Walker* was at the top of a UCLA study charting violence
in prime time series. But this characteristic only enhanced the
popularity of *Walker* among viewers. By 1995-1996, the third
season of the series, *Walker* topped all Saturday night shows,
averaging 19.4 million viewers and reaching 18th overall in
the weekly Nielsen ratings. *Walker, Texas Ranger* was at its

peak. The hit series would remain a significant part of Saturday night entertainment for years, and would encourage other films about Rangers during the 1990s.

The blockbuster success of *Lonesome Dove* in 1989 demanded sequels, although key characters—most notably Captain Gus McCrae—had been killed off. *Return to Lonesome Dove* was a 1993 mini-series which included several original cast members, including Rick Schroder. But Barbara Hershey replaced Angelica Huston, who chose not to return, while new characters were played by William Peterson, Oliver Reed, Lou Gossett, and Reese Witherspoon. Another new character, the

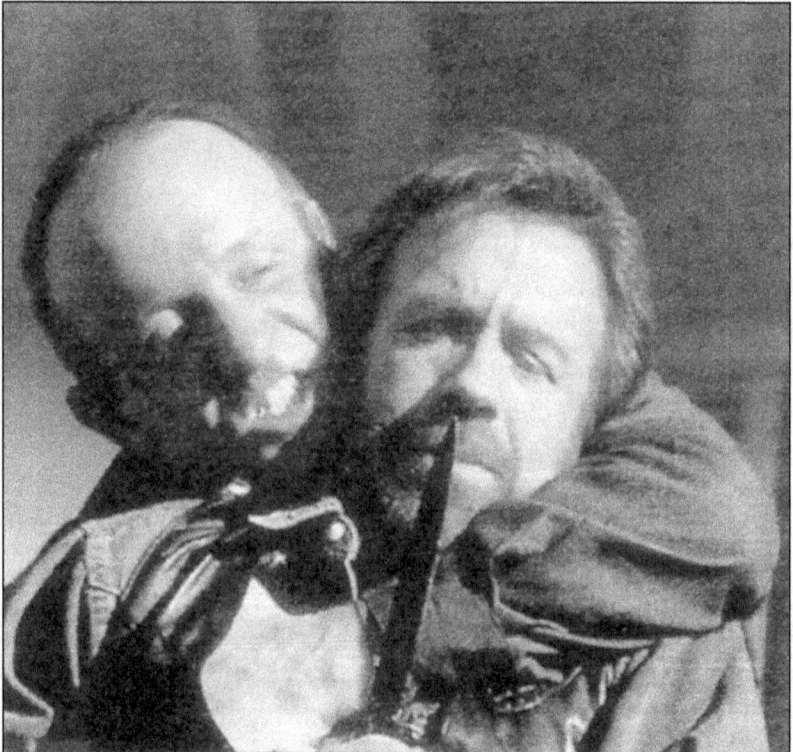

Ranger Cordell Walker (Chuck Norris) fights off a bad guy in an episode called "Deadly Reunion."

illegitimate daughter of Gus McCrae, was played by Nia Peeples, who later would join the cast of *Walker, Texas Ranger*, as a lady Ranger.

The key casting change involved the role of Captain Woodrow Call. The rugged, hard-bitten Call was memorably created by Tommy Lee Jones, who moved on to big screen projects. An excellent actor, Jon Voight had won an Academy Award in 1978 for *Coming Home*, and he had been nominated for Best Actor in two other years. He sported the same white beard as Jones in *Lonesome Dove*. But Voight lacked the raw power expected of Captain Call, and since Gus was dead, Call needed to carry the mini-series.

Return to Lonesome Dove begins with Call, having brought Gus back to Texas for final rest, rounding up a herd of wild horses for delivery to his Montana ranch. Call recruits one of his former Rangers, played by William Peterson, along with an eclectic group of horse drovers. Barbara Hershey remarks to Peterson: "I guess you're the final proof no one sane ever became a Texas Ranger." When confronted by various outlaws, both Peterson and Voight respond as if they still are Rangers. But most of the series occurs outside of Texas, and the Ranger connection is minimal.

Rangers and Ranger activities are far more prominent in the other two sequels to *Lonesome Dove*. In 1995 *Streets of Laredo*, based on Larry McMurtry's 1993 novel of the same title, offered "The Final Chapter" in the *Lonesome Dove* story. Longtime movie and television star James Garner assumed the role of Woodrow Call, now nearing the end of his career with a Ranger badge back on his vest. With his background in Westerns, Garner brought authority to the role of the manhunting old Ranger. But Garner's natural affability made it impossible for him to register Call's famous mean streak.

Streets of Laredo was filmed in Texas, and featured a trio of Texans in a superb cast. Sissy Spacek played Lorie (originally portrayed by Diane Lane in *Lonesome Dove*); Randy Quaid was menacing as John Wesley Hardin; and pretty Anjanette Comer was a disheveled prostitute in Crow Town. Sam Shepard was Pea, Captain Call's old Ranger companion, now married to Lorie (this unlikely couple has five children, and Lorie teaches at the one-room school near

James Garner took over the role of Woodrow Call, now a manhunter wearing his Ranger badge, in Streets of Laredo.

their farm). Ned Beatty was the colorful Judge Roy Bean, who held court from his Langtry saloon, which is faithfully reproduced. Pioneer cattleman Charles Goodnight was played by gravel-voiced James Gammon. Wes Studi was superb as a Kickapoo tracker, while comedian George Carlin was surprisingly effective—and unrecognizable—as a buckskin-clad frontiersman.

Streets of Laredo opens with Call preparing to ride in pursuit of kill-crazy Joey Garza, who has shot sixteen victims while robbing four trains. Joey shoots Judge Roy Bean, than hangs him from the porch of his saloon. (Bean died of natural causes in 1903—on the pool table in his saloon.) While reflecting upon his murderous prey, the old Ranger captain recalls that during twenty-four years of fighting Indians, he had lost only six men. Wherever he goes he is preceded by his towering reputation. "This here's Captain Call," explains a Texan to a newcomer. "He's the greatest Ranger that's ever been."

In a flashback scene, Ranger Call hangs Mexican horse thieves who are the grandfather and other ancestors of Joey Garza. Joey eventually guns down Call with a high-powered rifle. Lorie is forced to cut off Call's shattered leg. There are other grisly scenes and numerous killings before Joey finally is shot to death. *Streets of Laredo* is a grim and bloody story, its harshness unalleviated by the humor that Gus McCrae brought to *Lonesome Dove*. But throughout the *Streets of Laredo* the stellar qualities of Texas Rangers are extolled in various ways. In the final scene Charles Goodnight rides away from a visit with the crippled but game Call, and a cowboy observes, "I've always heard that he was the greatest Ranger of all."

This Ranger story was followed by another the next year. In 1995 Larry McMurtry published *Dead Man's Walk*, a prequel to *Lonesome Dove*, and in 1996 *Dead Man's Walk* appeared on television as a mini-series. Set in the Republic of Texas in 1842, *Dead Man's Walk*, like *Lonesome Dove*, weaves its tale around a long, dangerous journey. David Arquette plays a young Gus McCrae, while Johnny Lee Miller portrays his equally youthful partner, clean-shaven Woodrow Call. The

cast also includes Keith Carradine, Brian Dennehy, Edward James Olmos, Harry Dean Stanton, and F. Murray Abraham, winner of an Academy Award in 1984 as Best Actor in *Amadeus*.

Early in *Dead Man's Walk*, the youthful Call and Gus are Ranger recruits attempting to protect the Texas frontier. A veteran member of the company is legendary Ranger Big Foot Wallace, ably played by Keith Carradine. Brian Dennehy played the company commander, but he is killed in an Indian attack. In Austin the romantic Gus finds a sweetheart, but he and Call and Big Foot Wallace, among others, enlist in the Santa Fe Expedition. This ill-fated expedition set out from Austin to open trade with and take possession of Santa Fe, which Texas claimed was part of their Republic. But the expedition fell apart under the unexpected harshness of the Staked Plains and the assaults of Comanche raiders. The survivors of this terrible trek were captured by Mexican troops from Santa Fe.

In *Dead Man's Walk*, the survivors and their captors continue to struggle against weather conditions and Comanches. Eventually the surviving Texans are forced to draw beans; those who drew white beans would go free, but those who pulled out black beans had to stand before a firing squad. Big Foot Wallace was one of those who were executed. (Like Judge Roy Bean, Wallace actually died of old age, and the drawing of the black beans took place in the Mier Expedition south of the Rio Grande—but McMurtry always claims artistic license in large portions.) When the survivors finally struggle back to Austin, Call and Gus are veteran Rangers ready for further service. As Call tells Gus during one desperate situation: "Well, bein' a Ranger means you can die any day. You don't want to risk it, you oughta quit."

One survivor decides to quit, summing up an accurate description of Ranger work on the early frontier: "I guess this is where I quit the rangerin', boys. It's a rare sport, but it ain't quite safe."

The next year McMurtry produced *Comanche Moon*, another novel about the Ranger adventures of Gus McCrae and Woodrow Call. During a dozen years, 1985-1997, four McMurtry novels and four TV mini-series dramatized the lives of two Ranger captains. The impressions were so vivid that the library at the Texas Ranger Hall of Fame in Waco frequently was requested to produce the service records of Captain McCrae and Captain Call. When librarians replied that these captains were fictional Rangers, unbelieving patrons often insisted that Gus and Call were historic Rangers who simply must be in the archives!

Texas, a 1994 mini-series based on James Michener's epic novel of the same title, dramatized the creation of the Texas Rangers. The 1985 novel, published in two hardcover volumes totaling 1,185 pages, tells the story of Texas from 1535 until the 1980s. Michener covers a vast number of events by interweaving historical characters with generation after generation of fictional Texas families. Quite properly he devotes considerable attention to "one of the cherished symbols of Texas life" (p. 482), the Ranger force. During the 1820s Stephen F. Austin had created the idea of "ranging companies" as a means of protecting Texas settlers from hard-riding Comanches and marauding bandidos. The concept was revived when the Republic of Texas could not afford to maintain an army. Ranging companies would be formed to range and protect the countryside. There would be no uniforms, and each Ranger would provide his own horse and weapons.

Singer Randy Travis convincingly played a Ranger captain in the mini-series Texas, *then played a Ranger lieutenant several years later in the motion picture* Texas Rangers.

Michener told the story of the first Ranger company to patrol the lawless Nueces Strip, the vast area stretching from the Nueces River south to the Rio Grande. Michener's principal Rangers were: diminutive but deadly Otto Macnab, one of the main characters of the novel; San Jacinto hero Captain Sam Garner, seemingly a composite of captains Jack Hays, John S. "Rip" Ford, and Sam Walker; and gigantic Panther Komax, a fictional version of Big Foot Wallace. The Ranger nemesis in the Strip was Benito Garza, based on Juan Cortinas, the border hero famous among Mexicans as "Cheno." Michener described how the Rangers obtained the Colt Paterson revolvers, five-shooters which gave them repeating firearms that could be used on horseback.

In "The Ranger," a long chapter which ended the first volume of *Texas*, Michener sends Garner, Macnab and company into the War with Mexico, depicting Ranger exploits in considerable detail. In the second volume Ranger Macnab finally triumphs over Garza and, in a long career, over numerous other outlaws. When Macnab is murdered by a bushwhacker, five Rangers pursue the killer into Arizona Territory and riddle him with bullets. Macnab's son and grandson follow him into the Rangers. Michener also describes Captain M. T. "Lone Wolf" Gonzaullas in action in the rowdy oil fields of the 1920s.

The mini-series *Texas* reduced Michener's century-long storyline to just over two decades, from Stephen F. Austin's arrival in 1823 until Texas joins the United States in 1846. But the Rangers remain a focal point of *Texas*, concentrating on their activities in the Nueces Strip.

Texas boasted a strong cast, including Stacy Keach as Sam Houston, Patrick Duffy as Stephen F. Austin, and David Keith as perhaps the best Jim Bowie ever portrayed on film. The

deep, impressive voice of Charlton Heston provided narration. Singer Randy Travis, with a lean physique and a country accent that rings true for a Texas pioneer, plays Captain Sam Garner, while Rick Schroder bristles with determination as young Otto Macnab. Benjamin Bratt is effective as Benito Garza, border adversary of the Rangers.

Garner and Macnab march beside General Houston when Texas independence is won at San Jacinto. Soon Garner, Macnab and others volunteer when President Houston organizes "a new corps of men to be called the Texas Rangers. Men who are not tied to any one place, or any specific duties, outside of protecting the lives of every man, woman and child who lives here. So you'll range all over, especially around the borders." Houston added pointedly, "We do not have an army. You Rangers are all we've got."

Armed with Paterson Colts—rarely seen on film—the Rangers ride into battle against Benito Garza and his raiders. Otto finally slips into Garza's stronghold and kills his boyhood friend in a bloody shootout. Shot on location at Del Rio and Alamo Village, *Texas* offers the best film version of the Rangers' founding period, along with interesting combat scenes of the Alamo and San Jacinto.

Action superstar Bruce Willis headlined a 1995 motion picture that included a strong Ranger character. *Last Man Standing* was a remake of the Italian Western *A Fistful of Dollars*, which had made a star of Clint Eastwood. Set in the 1930s, *Last Man Standing* centered around a bootleggers' war in the fictional southwest Texas town of Jericho. Willis is a gunman who packs two .45 automatics in shoulder holsters and who sells his murderous services to both gangs. In the midst of the bloodbath an imposing Texas Ranger, Captain

In the violent Last Man Standing, *Bruce Willis hires his guns to rival boot-leggers in South Texas. But even Bruce seems intimidated when a tough Texas Ranger lays down the law.*

Tom Pickett, comes to Jericho and tells Willis and the sheriff that things are out of hand and he intends to return in ten days "with about twenty Rangers." Played with a quiet authority by Ken Jenkins, the captain assures Willis, "I believe in God, son." Wary of the captain's lethal promise to return to the force, the rival mobsters conclude the killing within the allotted number of days.

In 1995 the fifth film version of Zane Grey's *Riders of the Purple Sage* was released as a TV movie. There had been silent versions in 1918 and 1925, the latter starring Tom Mix. The sound versions were black and white B Westerns in 1931 and 1941, respectively, starring George O'Brien and George Montgomery. All of these movies were solid hits, including the 1941 film with a relative unknown starring as Lassiter. Grey's romanticized prose and long descriptive passages seem straight out of James Fenimore Cooper, and today are difficult to read and enjoy. But the best of Grey's characters and storylines radiate sheer power. When translated to the silver screen, the maundering prose is stripped away, replaced by action and Western scenery. *Riders of the Purple Sage* is probably Zane Grey's finest novel, and when reduced to a one-hour movie, Riders always proved forceful and compelling, with enough frontier romance remaining to exert primitive appeal.

More than half a century after George Montgomery's 1941 version, *Riders of the Purple Sage* was filmed as a vehicle for husband and wife actors, Ed Harris and Amy Madigan. Harris and Madigan were the most talented actors ever to play Lassiter and Jane, and the 1995 version was the only one of the five *Riders* to be lensed in color. Filmed in Utah, the desert vistas in Monument Valley are superb. Henry Thomas (*E.T.* and *Legends of the Fall*) is excellent as the sharpshooting cow-

boy, Bern Venters, who drills an outlaw, then is aghast to discover the masked rider to be a young woman. Venters nurses her back to health and they fall in love.

Following a long search, Lassiter (an ex-Ranger in previous films, although that background fact is not mentioned in this version) has come to Utah on the trail of the abductor of his dead sister, Milly. Lassiter intends to find her grave, and "to kill the men who persuaded Milly to abandon her home and her husband and her God." Wearing a two-gun rig, with a third revolver as a belly gun, Lassiter rescues Jane, falls in love, and kills of most of the bad guys. Wounded and pursued, Lassiter finally seals himself and Jane inside a hidden valley. The 1995 TV movie is the best of the five films about Zane Grey's finest book.

Another 1995 production, *Texas Payback*, focused upon retired Ranger Louis Gentry, now working in Las Vegas. When he still wore a Texas Ranger badge, Gentry had arrested killer Cody Giles. Giles escapes from prison and goes after Gentry in Las Vegas. The hackneyed plot is matched by the star power of Sam Jones (Gentry) and Gray Hudson (Giles), along with leading lady Kathleen Kinmont.

Of similar quality was a 1996 horror film which opened with a Ranger scene. *From Dusk 'Til Dawn* starred George Clooney, Quentin Tarantino, Harvey Keitel, and Selma Hayek. Michael Parks played a Texas Ranger named Earl. With a Western hat and wagon wheel badge and neat dress, Earl looks like a contemporary Ranger. But he is extremely foul-mouthed—hardly the wholesome image portrayed by Roy Rogers in *The Ranger and the Lady* or Clayton Moore in *The Lone Ranger*.

Ranger Earl begins the movie by entering a Big Spring

Who Was That Masked Man?

The first actor to play the Lone Ranger on film was Lee Powell, in a 1938 movie serial. The following year, a sequel serial starred Robert Livingston as the masked man. Klinton Spilsbury donned the mask in 1981 in *The Legend of the Lone Ranger*, and more than two decades later another tall, awkward actor, Chad Michael Murray, played the title role in a TV movie, *The Lone Ranger*.

But the most memorable image of this masked man was provided by Clayton Moore. An athletic actor in serials and other action movies, Moore landed the title role when The Lone Ranger became a television series in 1949. Except for a season when John Hart played the Lone Ranger, Moore wore the mask until the series ended in 1957. He also starred in Lone Ranger motion pictures in 1956 and 1958, and was seen thereafter in countless reruns of the TV series.

For the rest of his life Clayton Moore continued to appear in costume as the Lone Ranger, at rodeos and state fairs and mall openings. During the 1970s and 1980s, he would gallop into Arlington Stadium to introduce Texas Rangers baseball games, rearing his white horse at home plate. During a five-year legal challenge—ultimately unsuccessful—to stop him from wearing the trademark mask, Moore simply donned a pair of wraparound sunglasses to go with his Lone Ranger uniform.

"I never want to take off this white hat," said Moore to an Associated Press reporter in 1986. "When I take off to that big ranch in the sky, I still want to have it on my head."

Clayton Moore took off for that big ranch in the sky on December 28, 1999, at the age of eighty-five.

"When I go, I want them to say, 'Who was that masked man?'"

convenience store and, in his foul-mouthed manner, discussing a recent crime spree. The Gecko brothers (Clooney and Tarantino) have robbed a bank and have killed sixteen, including four Rangers. The tally soon rises to five Rangers, as the Gecko brothers step forward and murder Earl and the convenience store owner. The Gecko brothers flee to Mexico, where they encounter hideous vampires during their first night.

From Dusk 'Til Dawn became a cult classic and inspired two 1999 sequels, *From Dusk 'Til Dawn 2: Texas Blood Money* and *From Dusk 'Til Dawn 3: The Hangman's Daughter*. None of the stars of the original were present in the sequels, which both were set in Mexico (Number 3 was a prequel, set during the Mexican Revolution). Vampires abounded in both movies, but there were no Rangers.

There was a Texas Ranger moment in *The Newton Boys*, released in 1998. The movie told the story of four Texas brothers from Uvalde who robbed scores of banks during a five-year period, 1919-1924. (At the close of the film an elderly Willis Newton is shown in a taped interview, while Joe Newton drew huge laughs in an exchange with late-night king Johnny Carson). Native Texan Matthew McConaughey was excellent as Willis Newton. But Ethan Hawke, although a gifted actor, was too delicate to be convincing as the rugged cowboy, Jess Newton. *The Newton Boys* was filmed at Texas locations, and was colorful and exciting.

One scene written for Texas effect was the arrest of Jess Newton. Following a 1924 train robbery, Jess hid out in Mexico until postal inspectors tricked him into crossing the border, where he was arrested by the inspectors. In the movie Jess was apprehended by the famed Texas Ranger captain,

In The Newton Boys *the brothers were played by (L to R): Ethan Hawke (Jess); Texan Matthew McConaughey (Willis); Vincent D'Onofrio (Doc); and Skeet Ulrich (Joe). Joe was arrested by Ranger Captain Frank Hamer.*

Frank Hamer. A tall and imposing man in real life, Hamer was played by an actor who was no taller than Ethan Hawke.

In 1999 the prolific and award-winning Western novelist, Elmer Kelton from San Angelo, released the first volume of what would become his "Ranger Series." *The Buckskin Line* opens with the 1840 Comanche raid on Victoria and Linnville, a massive strike in retaliation for the treachery of Texans at the Council House Fight in San Antonio. When the enormous war party heads back to Comancheria with captives, scalps, and two or three thousand stolen horses, they are struck at Plum Creek by determined pursuers led by "ranging companies" and "minutemen." A red-headed little boy, whose parents have been murdered in the raid, is recovered by Mike Shannon. Raised on the Texas frontier by Mike and his wife, "Rusty Shannon" will become the central character of the Ranger Series.

Mike Shannon frequently rides with ranging companies to defend the frontier against Comanche raiders, and he drills the concept of duty into Rusty. While still in his teens, Rusty joins the "buckskin line" of poorly paid ranging companies. "They had no uniform, no badge, not even an official name," remarks the author in his Prologue. Rusty rides the buckskin line throughout the Civil War, and with his experience and sense of responsibility it seems likely that his career as a Texas Ranger will not end with the close of this book.

During the late 1990s *Walker, Texas Ranger* continued to be a staple of Saturday night TV. Utilizing his popular image, Chuck Norris organized a Kick Drugs Out of America program. He made frequent anti-drug appearances in area schools and, acting as a reserve police officer, Norris accompanied a drug raid in Terrell. In 1998 he married Gina O'Kelley in a

Carrollton ceremony, and the couple would make their home at his ranch near Navasota.

Tragically, in January 1999 a stuntman from Cumby, Texas, died of a heart attack during filming. Later in the year Noble Willingham, the likeable East Texan who played C. D. Parker, left the show to run for Congress. His character was written out of the show, but Willingham lost a close election. Despite such problems, *Walker* remained the most visible vehicle of Ranger entertainment at the end of the twentieth century.

1990s

BEST RANGER MOVIES
Dead Man's Walk (1996—Keith Carradine)
A Perfect World (1993—Clint Eastwood)

BEST RANGER TELEVISION SERIES
Walker, Texas Ranger (1993-2001—Chuck Norris)

BEST RANGER BOOKS
Dead Man's Walk (1995—Larry McMurtry)
Comanche Moon (1997—Larry McMurtry)
Streets of Laredo (1993—Larry McMurtry)
The Buckskin Line (1999—Elmer Kelton)
The Legend Begins: The Texas Rangers, 1823-1845
(1996—Frederick Wilkins)
The Law Comes To Texas: The Texas Rangers, 1870-1901
(1999—Frederick Wilkins)

R.I.P.
Clayton Moore, 85 (1999)

RANGER EVENTS
In 1993 the Ranger force was increased from 94 to 99, including two women Rangers. Salaries and fringe benefits also were increased, and by 1996 the authorized strength of the force was expanded to 105.

Two lengthy standoff sieges, the so-called "Republic of Texas" near Fort Davis, and the Branch Davidians, near Waco, drew the efforts of nearly the entire Ranger force, in addition to other officers.

Into the 21st Century

"Boys, I may lead you into hell; but I'll get you out if you do exactly as I tell you to do."

—Captain L.H. McNelly to his
Ranger company in *Texas Rangers*

*A*s a new century began, *Walker, Texas Ranger* continued to reinforce Ranger traditions every Saturday night. Ratings had dropped, but Chuck Norris made numerous attempts to strengthen the series. In a 2000 episode, for example, Mark Cuban, colorful owner of the Dallas Mavericks NBA team, made an appearance, along with his magnificent mansion. In the season finale on March 20, 2000, Walker married longtime sweetheart Alex Cahill. To improve appeal with younger audiences, Chuck Norris added two young Rangers, Sydney Cooke (played by Nia Peeples, a pretty brunette) and a hunk named Gage (played by Judson Mills). Both newcomers were adept at martial arts; like Walker, Gage would holster his gun to kick-punch a bad guy he was about to arrest.

Despite such efforts, the series lost about two million viewers during the 1999-2000 season, and another two million in 2000-2001. Although *Walker, Texas Ranger* still averaged 10.4 million viewers during 2000-2001, the show dropped to No. 58 in the Nielsen ratings. "I was burned out seven years ago," laughed Chuck Norris, who actively led his production

crew. Norris decided to close the series at the end of the eighth season. A two-hour finale, in May 2001, included his expectant wife, Alex, going into labor in the midst of explosive crime actions.

Thanks to syndication *Walker* did not really end. There had been 203 episodes, and in syndication *Walker, Texas Ranger* now is a constant presence on daytime TV. For well over a decade, then, hour-long episodes of *Walker* have promoted the courage and sense of justice of Texas Rangers. And *Walker, Texas Ranger* has been an updated continuation of the hour-long Westerns that filled movie screens during the 1930s and 1940s. Television critic Ed Bark observed that each week Walker faced "a gang of drooling villains" or "a parade of snarling, black-hatted bad guys." Of course, the bad guys wore black hats during the 1930s and 1940s, and the villains of these Westerns were just as easily recognizable as Walker's foes. Although the cinematic Texas Rangers of the 1930s and 1940s did not practice martial arts, they were skilled with their guns and fists, and like Walker, they always got their man within an hour. During the 21st century, *Walker* continues to reaffirm the heroic image of Texas Rangers that was so vividly established by movies of an earlier era.

Elmer Kelton continued his Ranger Series, begun in 1999, with the publication of two historical novels in 2001. In *Badger Boy* Rusty Shannon, at the end of the Civil War, is an experienced Texas Ranger. "I always felt like I was doin' something useful, bein' a ranger," mused Rusty. "Something useful" on the Texas frontier in 1865 included dealing with outlaws and army deserters, as well as with Comanche raiders. During one Ranger pursuit Rusty rescues a little boy, Andy Pickard, who had lived with Comanches since his parents were killed

Ranger Sculpture

The public reservoir of memories about the Texas Rangers includes films, novels, paintings, history books, museums, poems—and sculpture. At the Texas Ranger Hall of Fame and Museum in Waco, a formidable Ranger statue stands guard outside, and another looms near the main exit inside. In San Antonio, at the Texas Rangers and Trail Drivers Museum, handsome sculptures flank the front entrance. On one side is a group of trail drivers and longhorn cattle; on the other side is a mounted Ranger leading a pack mule.

The most recent Ranger statue was erected a few years ago on the courthouse square at San Marcos, the seat of Hays County. The county was organized in 1843 and named after Captain Jack Hays, who at the time was battling Comanches with his small Ranger company, utilizing the new Colt revolvers that had just been introduced to Texas. The tall statue depicts Captain Hays astride a horse and brandishing a Paterson Colt.

Inside the lobby at Love Field, the busy Dallas airport, a towering contemporary Ranger looks down upon travelers. Ranger Captain Jay Banks served as model for the impressive statue, which because of its location is probably seen by more people than any other Ranger sculpture. The inscribed label at the base includes the legendary Ranger motto:

TEXAS RANGER OF 1960 "ONE RIOT ONE RANGER"

*Statue of
Captain Jack
Hays on the
courthouse
square in
San Marcos,
with the
Hays County
courthouse
in the back-
ground.*
—Photo by
Karon O'Neal

*On April 30, 1961, the "Texas
Ranger of 1960" was dedi-
cated in the lobby at Love
Field. Captain Jay Banks of
Dallas was the model, and the
legendary "One Riot—One
Ranger" was engraved on the
base.*
—Photo by
Berri O'Neal Gormley

in a raid four years earlier. Rusty himself had been recovered as a toddler by Rangers at Plum Creek, following the murder of his parents. After the Rangers are disbanded at the end of the war, Rusty takes Andy—named "Badger Boy" by the Comanches because of his combativeness—to his farm in southeast Texas. Then the story jumps to 1871, when Rusty rejoins an informal Ranger force to battle Comanches.

Kelton's Ranger Series resumes in 1871 in *The Way of the Coyote*. Texans continue to endure Reconstruction, plagued by the detested State Police and Governor E. J. Davis. Rusty Shannon and his feisty ward, Andy Pickard, clash with Comanches and outlaws, and at one point lose their farm to crooked Reconstruction officials. Rusty again leagues with a Ranger company to right various wrongs, and so does young Andy. Andy stealthily employs skills he learned from the Comanches—the way of the coyote.

In 2002 Rusty and Andy continue their adventures in *Ranger's Trail*. By the fourth volume of Elmer Kelton's Ranger Series, Rusty's accumulated adven-

Elmer Kelton, award-winning Western novelist from San Angelo, has penned five books in his Ranger series.

tures seem more like the travails of Job. His parents have been murdered; his foster parents have died; he has received various wounds during his Ranger service; and the girl he planned to marry after the Civil War instead wed a Confederate veteran. In *Ranger's Trail* Rusty regroups and is about to marry a younger sister, but she is shot and dies in his arms. He seeks vengeance against those responsible, finding needed camaraderie in a frontier Ranger camp. The action takes place in 1874, and Rusty and Andy are present when Austin is an armed camp during the ouster of Reconstruction Governor E. J. Davis. "This was the beginning of the glory years," stated Kelton in the Foreward of *The Way of the Coyote*, "when these hard-riding horsemen and their admirers spawned the larger-than-life legends of the Texas Rangers."

Andy enlists in a new Ranger company. "The ranger oath is a solemn obligation between you and the state of Texas, taken in the sight of God," states Andy's enlistment officer. "I don't know what God's punishment is if you break it, but Texas's punishment can be severe." After Rusty completes his retribution in a bloody shootout, he decides to retire to his farm. But Andy returns to the ranger camp and encounters his captain. "Welcome back, ranger."

The fifth volume of the Ranger Series, *Shadow of a Star*, will be published in 2004, shortly after the completion of this book, and will continue the adventures of Rusty Shannon, Andy Pickard, and other familiar characters. In all four books that have been published as of this writing, Elmer Kelton has employed a large cast of continuing characters. Since a number of characters are Comanches, Kelton offers large doses of the Comanche culture. The Ranger Series storylines emphasize that during the early decades of the force, Rangers were occu-

pied primarily against Comanche raiders rather than against lawbreakers. Texas Rangers rode principally as an informal frontier militia before they became a law enforcement body, and Kelton's books drive home this point. Each book provides rich historical and cultural background, as well as occasional humor, and the Ranger Series is both entertaining and inform-ative.

Another recent novel portrays Rangers during the Civil War. *Call To Glory: The Life and Times of a Texas Ranger* was written by Michael and Marilyn Gilhuly and published in 2001. Like Rusty Shannon, brothers Leroy and Carter Wiley remain with the Rangers to protect the Texas frontier after war breaks out between North and South. But when their younger brother is captured by Union soldiers, Leroy and Carter use their guerilla skills to rescue him from prison camp. Returning to Texas, the brothers then ride with Rangers against Comanche war parties. Also portraying the women who stay at home, *Call To Glory* is a solid addition to Ranger literature.

The historical literature of the Rangers was significantly advanced in 2002 by the publication of *Lone Star Justice, The First Century of the Texas Rangers*. The author, Robert M. Utley, is a distinguished Western historian who currently is working on a second volume, which will trace the modern decades of Ranger exploits. Utley's work was preceded in 2000 by the able Texas historian, Charles Robinson III, whose *The Men Who Wear The Star* offers a readable account of the Rangers with thoughtful interpretations. In 2001 a biography of one of the most famous of all Ranger captains, Leander H. McNelly, was produced by Ranger historian Chuck Parsons and Marianna E. Hall Little, a descendant of three Rangers.

During that same year a feature film, *Texas Rangers*, fo-

cused upon Captain McNelly. As a young man McNelly achieved the rank of captain during four years of Civil War service. During Reconstruction he was appointed one of four captains of the State Police. When the Texas Rangers were re-organized, McNelly agreed to captain a forty-man company. Although quiet-spoken, Captain McNelly was a ferocious leader of men in a lawless land.

"Boys, I may lead you into hell; but I'll get you out if you do exactly as I tell you to do." Young recruit George Durham

Texas Rangers *starred (L to R): Ashton Kutcher, James Van Der Beek, and Dylan McDermott as Captain Leander McNelly.*

recorded his captain's challenging words. "I'll never send you into battle, I'll lead you. All I ask any man to do is follow me."

They followed him into the Nueces Strip, where he battled the Mexican raiders sent by General Juan N. Cortina and such Anglo outlaws as the ruthless King Fisher. Cattle and horses were stolen and ranches were burned. Cattle baron Richard King gave material support to McNelly's Rangers. Captain McNelly summarily executed his adversaries, tortured captives to extract information, and at least twice led his men on raids into Mexico—in clear violation of international law. In 1877 McNelly left the Rangers, and before the year was out he died of tuberculosis at the age of thirty-three. Richard King built a large monument over his grave.

To dramatize McNelly's story, *Texas Rangers* showcased a number of young actors, including several from hit TV shows. Dylan McDermott (*The Practice*) played McNelly; James Van Der Beek (*Dawson Creek*, *Varsity Blues*) starred as a fictional character, Lincoln Rogers Dunnison from Philadelphia, whose family was killed by King Fisher's large gang. User Raymond (*The Practice*) played an African-American recruit from Texarkana (there were no black Rangers in the 1870s nor for many decades to come). Robert Patrick (*Spy Kids*) was lean and tough as Sergeant John Armstrong, a noted Ranger who actually rode as McNelly's sergeant. Young hunk Ashton Kutcher delivered a lively, scene-stealing performance as George Durham, while Rachel Leigh Cook (*She's All That*) provided romantic interest as the daughter of cattle baron Richard Dukes. Richard Dukes, the film's version of Richard King, was played by old pro Tom Skerritt. Music star Randy Travis, who was impressive as a Ranger captain in the 1994 mini-series

Texas, again was convincing as McNelly's lieutenant. Alfred Molina was a cartoonish villain as King Fisher.

The youthful, popular cast brought good looks and high energy to *Texas Rangers*, and there was a great deal of riding and shooting. The Rangers all wore wagon wheel badges, and McNelly's actions in Mexico at Palo Alto and Las Cuevas are staged. The credits claim that *Texas Rangers* is based on George Durham's book, *Taming the Nueces Strip: The Story of McNelly's Rangers*. But the screenwriters largely ignored the real story, and most of the movie is preposterous. King Fisher has a fort in Mexico that boasts a Gatling gun, along with tunnels which defenders can use to emerge behind their attackers. The movie opens in 1875 with McNelly digging his own grave, while lamenting the kidnapping by raiders of his wife and three sons ten years earlier (when McNelly died in 1877, he was surrounded by his wife, son and daughter—who never were kidnapped by anyone). After Richard Dukes feeds the Rangers and allows them to train at his ranch, King Fisher launches an attack and hangs the rancher. (Richard King died in San Antonio's Menger Hotel of stomach cancer in 1885.) And while the Mexican scenes were filmed south of the border in Durango, the Texas scenes were shot north of the border in Alberta, Canada; the lush green scenery of Alberta does not remotely suggest the harsh Nueces Strip country, dominated by cactus and mesquite. Despite the promise of an attractive cast and a previously unexplored Ranger subject, *Texas Rangers* is a disappointing movie. But it is encouraging that filmmakers still remain ready to put a Ranger story on the big screen.

On the small screen, The History Channel aired an hour-long documentary in 2003, "The Enforcers: The Texas Rangers." Also, The WB Channel planned a youth-oriented

version of *The Lone Ranger* as a replacement series. But after viewing the two-hour opening episode, WB executives decided instead to use *Black Sash*, a martial arts series, airing *The Lone Ranger* film as a one-shot TV movie. Tall, slender Chad Michael Murray (familiar to television fans from *Dawson's Creek* and *Gilmore Girls*) played the Lone Ranger, although the Reid brothers had their names changed, to Luke Hartman and his Ranger sibling Harmon (Harm Hartman), played by Sebastian Spence.

In The Lone Ranger, *filmed for The WB Channel, Chad Michael Murray (left) played the title role and Nathaniel Arcand was Tonto.*

Luke, a twenty-year-old Harvard law student, travels to frontier Dallas to visit Harm and his wife and son. Stepping off the stagecoach, Luke hurries to the rescue of a lovely Indian girl—Alope, sister of Tonto, played by Anita Brown. Alope is being roughed up by four cowboys, who then rough up Luke until called off by their trail boss. When Harm leads a squad of Rangers in pursuit of a band of bad guys called "The Regulators," Luke tags along, only to be gutshot during an ambush. Harm and the other Rangers are killed and, adhering to established Lone Ranger formula, Tonto rescues Luke.

It seems that Tonto, played by young Nathaniel Arcand, remembers that Luke had tried to help his sister. Indeed, when Luke is taken to the tribal medicine tent, Alope helps Tonto remove the wounded man's clothing. Later a medicine man, played by the fine actor Wes Studi, aids Luke's recovery with a dose of peyote. While Luke is high on peyote, he envisions his dead brother and father, along with the superb white steed, Silver. During his reverie, Luke lounges in a hot mineral springs, where he fantasizes that Alope joins him, doffing her buckskins before entering the pool. From Tonto, Luke learns martial arts, with rock music throbbing in the background. Luke acquires a campy outfit, with raccoon mask, brown hat, shirt unbuttoned halfway down the front, and a gun rig which lacks silver bullets. The Lone Ranger and Tonto mount Silver and Scout and, under the admiring gaze of Alope, who is clad in an off-the-shoulder top with bare midriff, gallop away with the stirring strains of the William Tell Overture finally admitted to the soundtrack.

WB's updated version of *The Lone Ranger* apparently was too updated. It was hard to imagine Clayton Moore on a peyote trip or cavorting with a nude Indian maiden. Although crit-

ics and audiences scoffed at the latest *Lone Ranger*, it is reassuring that the old story continues to inspire remakes.

In the fall of 2003 filming took place in Austin on a motion picture entitled *Man of the House*. The movie stars native Texan Tommy Lee Jones, who co-starred as Captain Woodrow Call in *Lonesome Dove* and who won an Academy Award for his role in *The Fugitive*. Jones plays Roland Sharp, a tough Texas Ranger who is assigned an undercover role as an assistant cheerleading coach at the University of Texas to protect five cheerleaders who witnessed the murder of a federal informant. A scene was filmed at the Governor's Mansion, as Governor Rick Perry calls out the Rangers. ("With his Hollywood looks," laughed Governor Rick Perry's spokeswoman, Kathy Walt, "he was typecast to play the governor.")

Texas Governor Rick Perry has a cameo in Man of the House, *a 2005 action comedy starring Tommy Lee Jones as a crusty Ranger.*

In a delightful comedy performance, the rugged Jones courts a lovely English prof (Anne Archer) and saves the cheerleaders from various bad guys.

In the early years of the twenty-first century, a popular Ranger TV series is in constant reruns, a famed Ranger captain is dramatized in a feature film, the Lone Ranger is revived yet again on television, a noted Western novelist

is five volumes into his Ranger Series, and an Oscar-winning actor is starring on big screens as a contemporary Ranger. If some of the films have misfired, at least Texas Rangers still inspire creative efforts. The words on a Ranger statue in San Antonio suggest more than one promise for the future:

AS LONG AS THERE IS A TEXAS,
THERE WILL BE TEXAS RANGERS

Ranger statue outside the Texas Ranger and Trail Driver's Museum in San Antonio. Note the badge on the Ranger's vest. An inscription at the base of the statue reads: "AS LONG AS THERE IS A TEXAS, THERE WILL BE TEXAS RANGERS."

—Photo by Karon O'Neal

Western Stars and Ranger Movies

Most Western stars filmed at least one Ranger movie. Among actors who worked primarily in Westerns, the only major star who never made a Ranger film was Randolph Scott. Charles Starrett, who was voted one of Hollywood's Top Ten Western Stars for fifteen years, usually released one Ranger movie per year. Starrett starred in a total of fifteen Ranger films, more than any other actor.

Bob Allen
The Unknown Ranger (1936)
Rio Grande Ranger 1936)
Ranger Courage (1937)
Law of the Ranger (1937)
Reckless Ranger (1937)
The Rangers Step In (1937)

Broncho Billy Anderson
The Ranger's Bride (1910)
The Border Ranger (1911)

Gene Autry
Ride, Ranger Ride (1936)
The Big Show (1936)
Night Stage to Galveston (1952)
Winning of the West (1953)

Don "Red" Barry
Desert Bandit (1941)
Border Rangers (1950)

Johnny Mack Brown
Lawless Land (1937)
Rawhide Ranger (1941)
The Fighting Ranger (1948)

Gary Cooper
North West Mounted Police (1940)

Clint Eastwood
The Outlaw Josey Wales (1976)
A Perfect World (1993)

Wild Bill Elliott
The Law Comes to Texas (1939)
Vengeance of the West (1942)

Lone Texas Ranger (1945)
The Gallant Legion (1948)

Monte Hale
Ranger of the Cherokee Strip (1949)
South of Rio (1949)

Tim Holt
Renegade Ranger (1938)
Bandit Ranger (1942)
Come On Danger (1942)
The Arizona Ranger (1948)
Law of the Badlands (1950)

Buck Jones
Border Law (1931)
The Texas Ranger (1931)
Hello Trouble (1932)
The Fighting Ranger (1934)

Robert Livingston
The Lone Ranger Rides Again
    (1939)
Night Stage to Galveston (1952)
Winning of the West (1953)

Fred MacMurray
The Texas Rangers (1936)
Rangers of Fortune (1940)

Col. Tim McCoy
Code of the Rangers (1938)
The Phantom Ranger (1938)

Robert Mitchum
Border Patrol (1943)
Beyond the Last Frontier (1943)
The Wonderful Country (1959)

Tom Mix
The Ranger's Romance (1914)
The Lone Star Ranger (1923)
The Last of the Duanes (1924)
Riders of the Purple Sage (1925)
The Rainbow Trail (1925)
Outlaws of the Red River (1927)
The Miracle Rider (1935)

George Montgomery
The Lone Ranger (1938)
Riders of the Purple Sage (1941)
Last of the Duanes (1941)
The Texas Rangers (1951)

George O'Brien
The Lone Star Ranger (1930)
Last of the Duanes (1930)
Riders of the Purple Sage (1931)
The Dude Ranger (1934)
The Renegade Ranger (1938)

Tex Ritter
Vengeance of the West (1942)
Gangsters of the Frontier (1944)
Dead or Alive (1944)
The Whispering Skull (1944)
Marked for Murder (1945)
Enemy of the Law (1945)
Three in the Saddle (1945)
Frontier Fugitives (1945)
Flaming Bullets (1945)

Roy Rogers
Come On, Ranger (1938)
The Ranger and the Lady (1940)

Charles Starrett

The Mysterious Avenger (1936)
Outlaws of the Prairie (1937)
Riders of Black River (1938)
The Stranger from Texas (1938)
Two-Fisted Rangers (1940)
Riders of the Badlands (1941)
Riders of the Northland (1942)
Hail to the Rangers (1943)
Cyclone Prairie Rangers (1944)
Both Barrels Blazing (1945)
Roaring Rangers (1946)
Riders of the Lone Star (1947)
Bandits of El Dorado (1949)
Prairie Roundup (1951)
Ridin' the Outlaw Trail (1951)

Bob Steele

Trailin' North (1933)
Thundering Trails (1943)

Jimmy Wakely

Ridin' Down the Trail (1947)
The Rangers Ride (1948)

John Wayne

The Searchers (1956)
The Comancheros (1961)
True Grit (1969)

Bibliography

An important—and highly enjoyable—part of the research for *Reel Rangers* was viewing Ranger films. Almost all of the movies and most of the television episodes discussed in this book are available on video. Syndicated episodes of *Walker, Texas Ranger*, as well as various Ranger movies, frequently are telecast on cable TV. Also significant to the popular culture of Texas Rangers are the sculptures mentioned in the last chapter, as well as the museums in Waco and San Antonio (a number of other Texas museums have Ranger artifacts among their displays). The following books and articles also were helpful in compiling this volume:

Brooks, Tim, and Earle Marsh. *The Complete Directory of Prime Time Network TV Shows, 1946-Present*. Fourth Edition. New York: Ballantine Books, 1988.

Buscombe, Edward, ed. *The BFI Companion to the Western*. New York: Atheneum, 1988.

Campbell, Glen, with Tom Carter. *Rhinestone Cowboy*. New York: Villard Books, 1994.

Cox, Mike. *Texas Ranger Tales II*. Plano, Texas: Republic of Texas Press, 1999.

Davis, Ronald L. *John Ford, Hollywood's Old Master*. Norman: University of Oklahoma Press, 1995.

Dick, Barnard F., ed. *Columbia Pictures, Portrait of a Studio*. Lexington: The University Press of Kentucky, 1992.

Dunning, John. *Tune In Yesterday, The Ultimate Encyclopedia of Old-Time Radio, 1925-1976*. Englewood Cliffs, New Jersey: Prentice-Hall, Inc., 1976

Eckhart, Jerry. "Texas Ranger's Badge." *True West* (September 1993), 46-49.

Everson, William K. *A Pictorial History of the Western Film*. New York: The Citadel Press, 1969.

Eyles, Allen. *The Western*. New York: A. S. Barnes and Company, 1975.

Fehrenbach, T. R. *Comanches, The Destruction of a People*. New York: Alfred A. Knopf, 1974.

————, *Lone Star, A History of Texas and the Texans*. New York: The Macmillan Company, 1968.

Frost, H. Gordon, and John H. Jenkins. *"I'm Frank Hamer," The Life of a Texas Peace Officer*. Austin and New York: The Pemberton Press, 1968.

Garfield, Brian. *Western Films, A Complete Guide*. New York: Rawson Associates, 1982.

Gilhuly, Michael J. and Marilyn. *Call To Glory: The Life and Times of a Texas Ranger*. Marietta, Georgia: Longstreet Press, 2003.

Gossett, Sue. *The Films and Career of Audie Murphy*. Madison, N.C.: Empire Publishing, Inc., 1996.

Grey, Zane. *The Dude Ranger*. New York: Harper & Brothers, 1951.

————, *The Lone Star Ranger*. New York: Harper & Brothers, 1915.

————, *The Rainbow Trail*. New York: Harper & Brothers, 1915.

————, *Riders of the Purple Sage*. New York: Harper & Brothers, 1912.

Gruber, Frank. *Zane Grey, A Biography*. Roslyn, N.Y.: Walter J. Black, Inc., 1969.

Hardy, Phil. *The Western*. New York: William Morrow and Company, Inc., 1983.

Hirschhorn, Clive. *The Columbia Story*. London: Hamlyn, 1999.

————, *The Universal Story*. New York: Crown Publishers, Inc., 1983.

Holland, Tom. *B Western Actors Encyclopedia*. Jefferson, N.C.: MacFarland & Company, Inc., 1989.

Hurst, Richard Maurice. *Republic Studios: Between Poverty Row and the Majors*. Metuchen, N.J.: The Scarecrow Press, Inc., 1979.

An Illustrated History of the Texas Rangers. New York: Promontory Press, 1975.

Kelton, Elmer. *Badger Boy*. New York: A Tom Doherty Associates Book, 2001.

————, *The Buckskin Line*. New York: A Tom Doherty Associates Book, 1999.

————, *Lone Star Rising*. New York: A Tom Doherty Associates Book, 2003.

————, *Ranger's Trail*. New York: A Tom Doherty Associates Book, 2002.

————, *The Way of the Coyote*. New York: A Tom Doherty Associates Book, 2001.

McMurtry, Larry. *Comanche Moon*. New York: Simon & Schuster, 1997.

————, *Dead Man's Walk*. New York: Simon & Schuster, 1995.

————, *Lonesome Dove*. New York: Simon & Schuster, 1985.

————, *Streets of Laredo*. New York: Simon & Schuster, 1993.

Malsch, Brownson. *Lone Wolf, Captain M. T. Gonzaullas*. Austin: Shoal Creek Publishers, Inc., 1980.

Marill, Alvin H. *Robert Mitchum on the Screen*. New York: A. S. Barnes and Company, 1978.

Martin, Len D. *The Republic Pictures Checklist*. Jefferson, N.C.: MacFarland & Company, Inc., 1998.

Meyers, Jeffrey. *Gary Cooper, American Hero*. New York: William Morrow and Company, Inc., 1998.

Michener, James A. *Texas*. New York: Random House, 1985.

Moore, Clayton, with Frank Thompson. *I Was That Masked Man*. Dallas: Taylor Publishing Company, 1998.

Newton, Willis and Joe, as told to Claude Stanush. *The Newton Boys, Portrait of an Outlaw Gang*. Austin: State House Press, 1994.

O'Neal, Bill. *The Arizona Rangers*. Austin: Eakin Press, 1987.

————, *Tex Ritter, America's Most Beloved Cowboy*. Austin: Eakin Press, 1998.

O'Neal, Bill and Fred Goodwin. *The Sons of the Pioneers*. Austin: Eakin Press, 2001.

Parish, James Robert, and Michael R. Pitts. *The Great Western Pictures*. Metuchen, N.J.: The Scarecrow Press, Inc., 1976.

Parsons, Chuck, and Marianna E. Hall Little. *Captain L.H. McNelly, Texas Ranger*. Austin: State House Press, 2001.

Place, J.A. *The Western Films of John Ford*. Secaucus, N.J.: The Citadel Press, 1973.

Portis, Charles. *True Grit*. New York: Simon & Schuster, Inc., 1968.

Rainey, Buck. *Saddle Aces of the Cinema*. New York: A.S. Barnes & Company, Inc., 1980.

Ricci, Mark, and Boris and Steve Zmijewsky. *The Films of John Wayne*. New York: The Citadel Press, 1970.

Robinson, Charles M. III. *The Men Who Wear The Star*. New York: Random House, 2000.

Rothel, David. *An Ambush of Ghosts: A Personal Guide to Favorite Film Locations*. Madison, N.C.: Empire Publishing, Inc., 1990.

————, *The Singing Cowboys*. New York: A.S. Barnes & Company, Inc., 1978.

Sies, Luther F. *Encyclopedia of American Radio, 1920-1960*. Jefferson, N.C.: McFarland & Company, Inc., Publishers, 2000.

Terrace, Vincent. *Radio Programs, 1924-1984*. Jefferson, N.C.: McFarland & Company, Inc., Publishers, 1999.

Tuska, Jon. *The Filming of the West*. Garden City, New York: Doubleday & Company, Inc., 1976.

Utley, Robert M. *Lone Star Justice, The First Century of the Texas Rangers*. New York: Oxford University Press, 2002.

Webb, Walter P. *The Texas Rangers*. Austin: University of Texas Press, 1935.

Wellman, Paul I. *The Comancheros*. Garden City, N.Y.: Doubleday & Company, Inc., 1952.

West, Richard. *Television Westerns: Major and Minor Series, 1946-1978*. Jefferson, N.C.: MacFarland & Company, Inc., Publishers, 1987.

Wilkins, Frederick. *The Law Comes To Texas: The Texas Rangers, 1870-1901*. Austin: State House Press, 1999.

————, *The Legend Begins: The Texas Rangers, 1823-1845*. Austin: State House Press, 1996.

Index

About the Author

BILL O'NEAL is the author of more than thirty books, including numerous volumes on frontier history and Western movies. His titles on Western films include *Reel Cowboys*, *Tex Ritter*, and *The Sons of the Pioneers*. A recognized authority on the Old West, Bill has appeared on TV documentaries on The History Channel, TBS, The Discovery Channel, TNN, and A&E. He is a member of the Western Writers of America, and the National Association for Outlaw and Lawman History presented Bill their 2005 Book of the Year Award for *The Johnson County War*. Bill was selected as *True West* magazine's "Best Living Non-Fiction Writer, 2007."

www.ingramcontent.com/pod-product-compliance
Lightning Source LLC
Chambersburg PA
CBHW061300110426
42742CB00012BA/2000